"*The Four Pillars* rates among the best books on interpersonal selling. It presents sage wisdom with timely information in an easy to read format. It should be in every professional's library."

—*ROBERT LEOPOLD*
Regional Sales Director
3T Medical Systems

"Most of us who would like to think we are accomplished in the field of Medical Sales have the same classic sales books on our shelves, from Stephen Covey to Napoleon Hill and Harvey Mackay. Believe me when I tell you this book is destined to be on the shelf alongside them, written by a person who actually carried a bag, managed, owned, and later ran his own distributorships, and who now runs a major medical implant sales organization. This information is told and taught through experiences... not theory."

—*STEVE HUFF*
President
New England Medical Device

"*The Four Pillars of Sales* goes above and beyond, to truly break down the sales process from start to close—a must read! Insightful and very inspiring!

—*MJ MARASCO, Jr.*
Senior Institutional Sales Representative

"Gerry is the consummate sales professional. *The Four Pillars of Sales* shares decades of experience that will prove invaluable to those looking to sharpen their expertise and for those just getting underway. Well worth the read."

—*BILL McCARRICK*
Retired, Assoc. Dir. Connected Health
Zimmer Biomet

"This book by Gerry Savage, a successful medical device industry executive, contains invaluable content for us all. The "Four Pillars" in the title refers to attributes that all of us should strive to possess. They provide a foundation for life—both professional and personal. The book also contains important information about personality types, and the "steps in a sale" that have been proven necessary for success. Anyone interested in being in the sales profession should read this book."

—*RICK GERHART*
Owner
Kaizen Consulting, LLC

"*The Four Pillars of Sales* captures the timeless principles of Character and Leadership and describes for the reader how they can truly transform their destiny , both professionally and personally. Savage's stories are riveting. *The Four Pillars* is a must read for the salesperson who has the courage to make their dreams come true!"

—*ANDY KALAJIAN*
Founder and President
Fort Leadership and Sales Consulting

"The principles and approaches in Gerry's book are timeless. Not confined to theory but illustrated with his real life journey, you'll feel like you're riding alongside him on his calls. It doesn't matter if you are new to medical device sales or a seasoned veteran, his examples provide the blueprint for building a successful career....and lasting personal partnerships."

—*STEVE deBREE*
President
Performance Possibilities Group Inc.

The Four Pillars of Sales

Honesty, Integrity,
Knowledge, and Genuine Interest

GERRY SAVAGE

Year of the Book
135 Glen Avenue
Glen Rock, PA 17327

Print ISBN: 978-1-64649-028-8

Ebook ISBN: 978-1-64649-029-5

DEDICATION

I would like to dedicate this book to my mom and dad.

My dad was my hero, a legend in orthopedic sales from 1970 through the early '90s.

Mom was a great philosopher. She said, "Anything you learn is not lost," and "You can do anything you put your mind to." I believed her then and I believe her now.

My parents instilled in me a sound work ethic and a never-quit attitude. "Just do your best," they would always say. They encouraged me in anything I tried and stood by me through the good times and the bad. Even now as they have since passed, I can hear their voices of support. I hope they would be proud of this book.

Contents

INTRODUCTION

My dad was a salesman. Like many parents, he wanted me—his oldest son—to follow in his footsteps. After getting released from active duty in the Marine Corps in 1985, I went to work for him in orthopedic sales. I was twenty-four and for the previous four years I had gone wherever Uncle Sam told me to go, and did what I was told to do.

With little to no sales training—and walking in the shadow of a giant in the industry—I didn't make the grade. After six months I quit.

I hate that word, because I'm not a quitter. Instead, I got a job selling cars and became successful, working my way through the ranks up to a desk manager and sales coordinator for the SAAB product line at a Portland dealership in Maine.

In 1991, with more experience in automobile sales (and enough rejection for a lifetime), I went back to work in orthopedic sales. In fact, I stayed with Zimmer Orthopedics for eight years as a sales representative and won five prestigious President's Club awards. Then in the early 2000s, I became a Biomet distributor and later returned to Zimmer in 2006 to manage the Trauma portfolio of a $100M distributorship. During that time, I earned my MBA from Eastern University where I later became an adjunct professor. In 2012 I was hired as Regional Sales director in the eastern U.S. for Conformis, a company that was the first to bring a completely customized knee replacement to market. In 2017, I accepted the position of east region Vice President for MicroPort Orthopedics and in 2019 became Vice President of Sales U.S. for Maxx Orthopedics.

So, how do I get to work with you and help you reach and achieve the level you desire for *your* sales career? There are thousands of sales books out there to choose from, and quite frankly everyone has something to say. Several authors want to give you the impression that if you just follow the steps, their method will bring you all the success you desire. But the truth is, no one has all the answers. I hope you will read this book over and over and mark it up with notes. I also hope you will read other books, articles, and anything you can get your hands on. Attend seminars, model yourself after people you know have achieved the success you're craving. At any age or any point in your career, the key is to stay relevant.

Become a lifelong learner. I am still learning after all these years, and my gift to you is to give you something you can use—another arrow in your quiver, another valuable tool in the toolbox, or an experience that gives you a thirst to understand more about people and to want to learn more every day.

Create a relationship, not a sales pitch.

But beware of chasing shiny objects. I encourage you to question each new tool for relevance before you embrace it. When you pick up a book, for example, read the back cover to see if it captures your interest. If the topic is relevant—for career or personal growth—then look for a connection to the author or the content, and decide if it can be easily read and understood.

Give it my "three bears test": Is the porridge too hot, too cold, or just right? I hope you find this book is just right.

Remember, life is a journey. By selecting this book *and reading*, you are demonstrating that you want success in your sales career. One book will never give you all the answers, however. It is my hope to provide you with a foundation and framework that propels you to the next level of your career, whether you're just starting out or ready to break through a perceived ceiling.

If someone had asked what I wanted to be when I grew up, "salesman" wasn't even on the radar, and my guess is that you would say the same thing. Personally, I wanted to be a pilot. I started flying airplanes when I was just sixteen years old, and after two years of college I joined the Marine Corps because they still had enlisted flight navigators on C130 transports. All I wanted to do at that point in my life was fly.

As my mother always told me, the great thing in life is that "nothing you learn is lost." In fact, whether you like it or not, that information gets tucked away somewhere in your brain, and you would be surprised what can trigger a memory at some future point—a smell, a taste, even the opening chords of a song you haven't heard in years.

The sales lessons in this book intentionally incorporate stories from my life and experience. You will discover that when you learn to share similar stories from your own perspective later, this is what can drive and deepen connections with your prospects and clients as your career blossoms. By the time you finish reading, I hope you will find yourself incorporating your own life experiences effectively in almost any situation—sales or otherwise.

Through these pages you will discover that sales will flow almost effortlessly when you engage with your customer and take their preferred work/personality style into consideration, creating a relationship rather than a pitch. Don't worry... you have more to talk about and more to share than you realize.

Your career will likely have struggles along the way. I have made more mistakes and failures than I care to mention, but that's okay, because I believe these so-called mistakes are merely lessons that require us to make course corrections. Even subtle shifts create huge change.

Michael Jordan once said, "I've missed more than 9,000 shots in my career. I've lost almost 300 games. Twenty-six times, I've been trusted to take the game-winning shot... and missed. I've failed over and over and over again in my life. And that is why I succeed."

Similarly, NFL Hall of Famer Brett Favre threw 336 passes that resulted in interceptions, but when you take into consideration that number was reached by way of 10,169 total passes—6,300 of them completed—his success is obvious.

In his book *A Better Way to Live*, the famous author Og Mandino talks about how he once called the public relations department at the Atlanta Braves in 1974 when Hank Aaron was about to break Babe Ruth's home run record. At the time, Hank had 710 home runs and only needed five more to surpass Babe Ruth. Og wanted to know how many strike-outs Hank had. To that point in his career lifetime, Hank had 1262 strikeouts. The most successful hitter in history had struck out almost twice for every hit. This quote from OG Mandino is something we should all remember.

"Life is a game with rules that must be followed in order to triumph, but you don't have to hit a home run every time you come to bat in order to be a success in this world. Ask Hank." ~OG Mandino

---

Failure is a part of winning. Failure is required in order to become successful. Such failure is a part of life. Stats are fun to debate, but the successful athlete, the successful manager, the successful CEO, and the successful salesperson will all tell you they have failed over and over. But the only way you can truly fail... is if you stop trying.

Sometimes the problem is that you can't see the goal line. We imagine it at some distant unobtainable point on the horizon, however it may be only a step or two away. Never stop; just keep putting one foot in front of the other. You don't have to see the whole staircase. Together let's take a few steps and get you closer to that goal... whatever it is for you.

I've heard world renowned life coach and bestselling author Tony Robbins say in his program Personal Power, "Success leaves clues," and you can find them everywhere...

Becoming better in sales is just one small piece of creating a life more meaningful than you ever dreamed. Use the knowledge you find here to bring yourself to new heights. It may be crowded at the bottom, but the view from the top is breathtaking.

"The Journey of a thousand miles begins with one step." ~Lao Tzu

---

PART ONE

Getting Ready

CHAPTER 1

THE FOUR PILLARS

"Live, love, laugh, learn, and leave a legacy."

~Stephen Covey

The foundation of this book is built around what I like to call the "Four Pillars of Sales." If you are standing on a firm foundation ready to build your sales career, or even remodel it, renovations can be a good thing. But what's holding up the roof?

The inspiration for the Four Pillars came from the awe-inspiring Parthenon in Greece. Built almost 2,500 years ago as a temple to the Goddess Athena, it has stood the test of time and is the most visited archeological site in the world.

Metaphors are everywhere in life and I'm sure you have heard that "your body is your temple," and "you are what you eat." I believe this all to be true, and the more good things you put into your body, the more good things will come out. If you eat right and exercise, your body will become fitter, you will feel better about yourself, you will have more energy, and as a result you will do more. When you do more, you feel more accomplished. The benefits go on and on.

We all need to take care of the foundation—your body and your mind—because everything you do, achieve, accomplish, and learn is housed inside. What's holding up the roof makes all the difference.

The Four Pillars of Sales are *honesty, integrity, knowledge,* and *genuine interest,* and these will not only hold up your roof, but will protect your firm foundation and allow you to fill your house with everything you need to enrich your sales career—as well as your life—and cement your legacy for generations to come.

The pillar of *honesty* is something people will see in you as a result of your actions on a regular basis. Everything we do is noted by those with whom we interact. Honesty means telling the truth, but it also means doing what you say you will do. The actions have to follow the words.

Years ago when I was in automobile sales, my general manager told me something that has continued to resonate. "The mark of you is what you do... not what you say you will do." Lip service will never get you anywhere and it will catch up with you sooner than you think.

We all get pressed for deadlines and—even with good intentions—we over-commit and under-deliver. Being honest starts with being honest with yourself. It means accepting responsibility for your actions and not placing blame on others.

What's holding up the roof makes all the difference.

We can all come up with a story about why we failed at something or why something didn't go our way, but deep down we know whether we gave it our all, doing the best we could possibly do. We have no control over outside circumstances. The only thing we can control is how we respond... and that starts with being honest with ourselves.

The second pillar of *integrity* is often referred to as "doing the right thing when no one is looking," but it's much more than that. Integrity is a bold word and when you see someone that you know has a lot of integrity, how do you feel about them?

For me, I feel like I can count on this kind of person. If they have high integrity, I am more likely to trust them. I know they will do the right thing when no one else is looking, and I know they will do what's in the best interest of everyone involved. This goes for every person they come into contact with... at work, home, in a volunteer group, or anywhere there is a responsibility, whether it be completing an action or representing the best interest of others.

Someone of high integrity also automatically treats others the way they would want to be treated. There is no in-between. They believe everyone has something to offer. One person is just as important as the next. A friend of mine and former colleague at Zimmer Orthopedics epitomizes this. He is someone who listens intently to understand, has always been there for sound advice, and has never said a cross word about anyone. You can already begin to see why someone of high integrity is well thought of and looked up to by others, especially this individual.

The third pillar of *knowledge* is critical. You have heard before that "knowledge is power." You can have all the other pillars intact but without knowledge, your house will not be fully supported.

There are more ways to increase knowledge today than ever before. Just thirty years ago I accomplished this by listening to cassette tapes in my car. We didn't have such things as podcasts, or the internet. We didn't have Kindles, and you couldn't Google a quick fact about anything in a millisecond. You actually had to read it somewhere, and probably look it up.

Times sure have changed. Now we have even less room for excuses than ever before. It is almost easy to increase our knowledge on a daily basis. Truly amazing, there is so much right there at our fingertips. All we have to do is reach out and touch it.

The more you learn each day, the more you will be able to use this knowledge. You will be surprised how much of what you consider random facts can come up in everyday conversation, as well as in sales calls. Used respectfully in any conversation, such knowledge in a particular area can set you apart, and in a sales situation, it will give you an edge above all the competition.

If you continue to increase your knowledge of the world and your industry on a daily basis, I can almost guarantee it will make a difference in how others perceive you.

The mark of you is what you do... not what you say you will do.

The fourth pillar of *genuine interest* is the one that will connect you with more people than you ever dreamed, and the more you connect, the more you will learn. It will perpetually increase your interest in people, expanding your horizons and areas of interest tenfold.

When people sense you are genuinely interested in them, they will become more likely to embrace you and your thoughts and ideas in return. It's reciprocal. People will not only sense that you have genuine interest in them, but they will sense that you are genuine as well.

Everyone has something to offer and taking the time to be genuinely interested in a person will open the door to relationships you never imagined.

WHAT IS SALES?

Did you ever stop to wonder... *just what is sales?*

Is it someone agreeing to buy something? Is it exchanging one thing of value for something else of value? Is this transaction getting the customer something they need, or merely fulfilling what another person wants?

The definition of sales gets pretty convoluted, but it also means helping a customer realize there are products or services available that can make their job easier. Sales then becomes the process of helping a customer decide how to fulfill this need they have with a particular product or service.

But that product or service has a *potential value* as well as a *perceived value* based on the buyer's need, the seller's product availability, and market pressure driven by similar products/services (the competition).

When I was a kid back in the early 1970s, my dad sold orthopedic soft goods as part of his product portfolio. These included things like slings for fractured arms, knee immobilizers to keep a patient's leg straight after surgery, and cervical collars for neck injuries. He would try these things on me to make sure he knew how to demonstrate them to the nurses and staff at his hospital accounts. It was pretty comical at times standing there with a cervical collar on my neck, a sling on my arm, and a knee immobilizer wrapped around my leg.

Back then these soft goods were worth the time to demonstrate and sell because they were high-volume items—and commissions were good. Fast-forward just ten years later and the market for these types of products drastically changed. How? Soft goods became a commodity. Price became dictated by what the market would bear—driven down by standardized mass-market products, and many companies who produced the same thing.

Eventually if a salesman was able to get a soft goods contract at a hospital, it was for nearly the entire line of soft goods... but at a low price. These soft goods became a loss leader for a company, and so the salesman earned very low commission rates. Demonstrating or detailing these products has since become a thing of the past.

Many experienced salesmen will tell you that sales has always been a relationship business, and this holds true over time. Even in today's price-sensitive world, relationships are the key to gaining new business, sustaining current business, and protecting future business.

Other factors in many industries have inched their way into the sales environment. In the medical device world, value analysis committees at the hospital level, as well as group purchasing organizations that partner with several hospitals to leverage price, now play a major role in determining what products are used. In addition, because of economic pressures, many surgeons have opted to become hospital employees, thus relinquishing much of their control over what company, product, or implant they use. What ways have economic pressures affected your industry? And how has that changed the way you do business?

While there are several factors that affect every industry and the sale of products or services, selling still boils down to the exchange of a product or service for something of value. What precipitates a sale is the creation of that long-lasting customer relationship built on the Four Pillars of *honesty, integrity, knowledge,* and *genuine interest.*

The interesting thing—and one of the complexities of selling today—is that everyone wants to control an account not only for its sales and volume, but for control of the buying relationship. When I say *relationship,* I mean the person or entity in control of what product or service is ultimately selected. For years in orthopedics, surgeons were the ones who determined what product they wanted to use. They were the ones performing the surgery and they could make the argument that one product—in this case, the implant for a hip or knee replacement—had specific advantages and worked better in their hands. Today, in many instances, control over product selection has been taken from the surgeon because the hospital wants to drive down the cost of implants.

Relationships are the key to gaining new business, sustaining current business, and protecting future business.

While the increase of surgery in the Ambulatory Surgery Center (ASC) has created an extension of the market, it has also created even more price sensitivity. The rising cost of care and decrease in reimbursements to physicians and hospitals by Medicare continues to drive implant costs even lower. The double-edged sword is that companies need to innovate now more than ever; however, the task is daunting. How is this true in your industry?

In today's competitive environment of decreasing revenue streams, it now becomes more about access to an account. If a company has access to an account via a group contract, then it becomes incumbent on the salesperson to gain the business. In many instances, contracts have become dual-source—meaning two vendors—or involve a certain price cap.

In my experience, sole-source contracts can occur and could be a major disadvantage to a hospital, surgeon, and ultimately the patient. I do not believe one company has everything for everyone, and I also believe it's important that a surgeon has access to whatever is needed to ensure the best possible outcome for the patient. This is just my bias, but it's based on over 30 years in the medical device industry.

As your sales career unfolds, remember to pay attention to not only the basic tenets of your industry, but also the trends that shape and re-shape how your customers make decisions. There is a saying that "What got you here won't get you there." As the way your customers make decisions and as their buying process changes and evolves, so too must you be willing and able to adapt.

FINDING COMMON GROUND IN SALES

The best sales processes are built on strong relationships that develop because of mutual trust and respect. These can only be built on a foundation of common ground.

The answer to finding common ground quickly lies in connection; you must be able to communicate effectively in order to build any type of relationship. In later chapters, you will learn how to use personality types—both yours and your prospect's—to make this process easier. I'm not suggesting that you will become able to effectively communicate with everyone or that you will be able to build a relationship with every prospect you meet. As you already know or have figured out somewhere along the way in your life, not everyone is going to like you... and certainly not everyone is going to agree with you all the time. The same should be true for you in business. You are not going to like everyone you meet, and you are not going to agree with everything someone else has to say.

Here is a news flash: Even though someone is not going to buy from you now... you should still respect their decision. Just because someone doesn't buy from you today doesn't mean they won't buy from you tomorrow or a year from now.

> **Just because someone doesn't buy from you today does not mean they won't buy from you tomorrow or a year from now.**

Respect comes from—and is built upon—the Four Pillars of *honesty, integrity, knowledge,* and a *genuine interest* in the other person's (the customer's) needs. If you understand that person's needs, you are in essence helping them solve a problem. Even if you may not be able to help them immediately, you will have laid the groundwork and built your relationship on a solid foundation, which may bring even bigger opportunities down the road.

When I was a young orthopedic sales rep in Bangor, Maine, I would drive to Eastern Maine Medical Center several times a week and wait in the orthopedic clinic to speak with surgeons as they came in to take a break between cases or to see patients. I didn't have much business at all in those days, but even so, when I went to the clinic I tried to be respectful of the surgeons' time. Instead of leaping into a sales spiel, I endeavored to show them I wanted to learn and that I wasn't going anywhere. Often in sales, respect is earned by resiliency.

Over time as I began to build business, it filtered back to me from another well-respected rep that one of the surgeons saw me as "relentless" and "tenacious." In this case, he meant it as a compliment, so be cautious of jumping to conclusions if someone labels you in the future. This surgeon took me under his wing and I am grateful for all I learned from him. I knew these surgeons respected me, and since I respected their time, they came to see me as someone who wouldn't quit. I think that's a great trait for anyone to have. Never give up! You may be just a couple of steps away from the goal line.

Though *relentless* and *tenacious,* I still didn't have much total joint replacement business with my biggest account. At the time, they had twelve surgeons doing trauma and total joint replacement cases. I visited frequently but because I respected their time, I tried never to overstay my welcome. The trauma cases were very service-intensive, and eventually I was able to land many of them.

Because trauma cases often came in the middle of the night, I spent many nights in the operating room with the surgeon on call because he/she was happy to have my help, and of course use my intramedullary nail or plate to fix a fracture. While waiting for these cases to start, I would (at the appropriate time) have subtle conversations about my knee or hip system. As a result, over time, I became experienced at trauma and the operating room staff as well as the surgeons began to rely on me more and more. The relationships we talked about building earlier began to take shape because they trusted me and they all began to speak about this amongst themselves.

After a long night fixing a fractured femur, a surgeon told several other surgeons sitting in the orthopedic clinic that I had been incredible the night before, helping him and the operating room staff on call. This surgeon had never used one of my total knee systems, but not too long afterward, I received a personal call from him. "Hey, I had a case booked with the new DuPuy rep and he didn't even know I used his system; I'm using yours on my next case. When can we go over the instruments?" It was humbling to me that this surgeon who had many other options would give me such an opportunity. That case went very well, and so I got all his total knee cases after that first one.

By establishing a deeper connection with one prospective client at a time, rather than shallow or surface-only connections to many, it ultimately led to sales success. Consider ways in your industry that will allow you to connect more strongly with your prospects, and watch the word-of-mouth referrals pay future dividends.

Connect deeper and watch referrals skyrocket.

A close friend in New England worked for three major orthopedic companies over the last twenty years. We were fierce competitors in the beginning, and both developed strong relationships with our surgeon customers within the territory we shared. As you may guess, we were not friendly while we were competing, although we did develop mutual respect. It was only years later after I left the area that we connected and became close. I share this story to show the importance of relationships—not the relationship I have with him, but the ones he established with his customers. Each of the three times he switched companies for a better position, his customers wanted to switch with him. This is extremely difficult to accomplish. So we must return to our initial question: *What is Sales?*

In any industry, sales is the exchange of something of value. It is based on several factors beginning with the *need* for a product. *Price, product availability, market pressure*, and who has *control* over the buying process, all play a major role in growing business for any company, and helping a customer to come to a decision based on a need they have for your product or service. Beyond all of this though is the relationship built between you and your prospective customer.

Ron Willingham, in his book *Integrity Selling* said, "Sales is something you do for and with someone, not to someone."

Remember the *Four Pillars:*

- *Honesty*
- *Integrity*
- *Knowledge*
- *Genuine interest*

A relationship built on these principles will serve you well throughout your career. Make them part of your everyday life so that each and every thing built on this firm foundation will stand the test of time. Even sales that don't come your way today may come to you tomorrow. Stay the course, and stay true to these Four Pillars, and you will get that phone call saying, "I want to do business with you."

SUMMARY

- Sales is an exchange of a product or service for something of value (time, money, etc.).

- It is based on a need of the customer.

- It is a process of helping the customer uncover and solve that need, and come to a decision on the product or service.

- Long-lasting customers come from forming strong relationships.

- Relationships are built on the Four Pillars of *honesty, integrity, knowledge,* and *genuine interest.*

- "Sales is something you do for and with someone, not *to* someone."

"Relationships are the hallmark of the mature person."
~Brian Tracy

Chapter 2

It All Starts With a Dream

Too many people die young—even before their physical death. What I mean is that we all have dreams, but unfortunately some let those dreams die... and with them go their hopes, ambitions, and minds. That is a tragedy.

Those who follow through with their great dreams see not only benefit for themselves, but for others as well. You should know that everything you do or say in life will affect other people. That effect may be positive or negative. My hope is that you will be among those who pursue your dreams in a positive way and find joy through the accomplishment.

The realization of your dreams will in turn fuel your innermost drive, and from there you can and will accomplish more. Never stop dreaming and never take those dreams lightly. Reach down deep inside and begin to ask yourself questions that will give you the success you most desire.

What is it you want to achieve in your sales career and your life?

If you view life as a game, where would you rather be: in the bleachers watching, or on the field playing the game? Generally speaking, the ones on the field are earning a whole lot more than the spectators.

So what is your dream? What is it you expect to accomplish in your sales career? I know you're searching, or you wouldn't be here with me.

Asking Better Questions

Asking better questions is a call to action. It takes your dream from inside your mind, out of the bleachers, and on to the playing field. It gets you smack dab in the middle of this game of life. For any question you ask yourself, your brain will provide an answer... so it's imperative that you're asking the right questions.

Would you rather be in the bleachers watching, or on the field playing the game?

Banish thoughts like: "Why does this always happen to me?" Instead ask: "How can I turn this situation into a positive experience?"

Instead of telling yourself "I'm such a loser, I never get it right," ask, "What can I learn from this experience that will make me better?"

If you dream of becoming the top sales professional in your company, then stop asking yourself, "Why do I always have bad months?" and instead affirm, "Every month my sales will get stronger."

We don't have an owner's manual for that runaway computer inside our heads, so we must be careful what we ask it! At first, your brain may give you only negative answers since that is the outcome you have trained yourself to expect. But your brain can also give you the positive outlook you're looking for, if you just start searching in a different direction.

To consistently find answers that will drive and motivate you, begin phrasing your questions like: "How can I accomplish that goal?" and "What steps do I need to take to close that account?"

Framed in this positive approach, your new questions will instantly move you beyond the "I hope I can do this" hurdle. "I will" goes much further than "I hope."

The new questions will have brought you to a place where your mind springs into action and gives you the answers you require to physically pull off whatever task or challenge you're facing.

Wouldn't you agree this is a much better starting place than "Why does this always happen to me?" or "I hope I can do it"? I think so, too!

In his book *Think and Grow Rich*, Napoleon Hill introduced the power of auto-suggestion. Auto-suggestion implies that by writing down positive thoughts and affirmations and repeating them daily, they will cause you to believe in yourself, and in turn, others will believe in you also.

> "Like the wind which carries one ship East and another West, the law of auto-suggestion will lift you up, pull you down, according to the way you set your thought."

Hill goes on to quote Walter D. Wintle's poem, *Thinking*, to demonstrate the power of auto-suggestion.

If you think you are beaten, you are
If you think you dare not, you don't,
If you like to win, but you think you can't
It is almost certain you won't.

If you think you'll lose, you're lost
For out of the world we find,
Success begins with a fellow's will
It's all in the state of mind.

If you think you are outclassed, you are
You've got to think high to rise,
You've got to be sure of yourself before
You can ever win a prize.

Life's battles don't always go
To the stronger or faster man,
But soon or late the man who wins
Is the man WHO THINKS HE CAN!

THE BEST IDEAS CAN COME OUT OF FAILURE

When I sit back and reflect on where and when I've found my best ideas, it has usually been shortly after a major failure or following a serious or tragic event. Now I am not advocating failure or tragic events as a means of shaping your future, but the fact is, history shows that highly successful individuals frequently had to overcome huge obstacles in order to do great things.

Take Ray Charles, for instance—a man born with sight who lost it. Ray overcame other challenges such as drug addiction, but what would have become of him if he had simply withdrawn inside himself and never pursued his love of music? If Ray had spent all his time asking, "Why did this happen to me?" do you think we would ever have had the pleasure of hearing him perform?

Stop asking questions that guilt and belittle yourself.

Remember, everything you do affects someone else! I can't even begin to calculate the effect Ray Charles must have had on others—other musicians, those who suffered addiction, those affected by vision loss. What a positive role model!

If you've found yourself stuck after the loss of a job, the loss of a key account, or the loss of a bid, the question I pose to you is: "What question will you ask yourself next?"

When you stop asking questions that guilt and belittle yourself, and instead ask the right questions framed in a more positive light, you will finally begin to rise to new and greater heights. Why? Because rather than wallowing in the negative, you will have become strong enough to assess what happened, then internalize the pain, take responsibility, and recognize that you never want to be in that place again.

If you continue to believe that life is a process, you will continually learn from both the good and the bad experiences.

Fortunately, those unpleasant ones are what usually cause us to dream bigger and strive for higher goals. A life in sales can sometimes feel like a rollercoaster ride filled with peaks, valleys, hairpin curves... and rapid rises and descents.

As Dennis Waitley says in his program, *The Psychology of Winning*, "Through adversity comes the call to greatness, while often through complacency comes the lull of apathy." Answer the call to greatness in your own life.

CHOICES AFFECT MORE THAN JUST YOU

In 2006, I was offered a position as sales director in another state. The next year I moved my family so I could pursue this dream and desire to further my career. It was a gut-wrenching decision... one I made with my family.

You can imagine the turmoil our oldest daughter felt when she had just finished her senior year and moved away days later. Our middle daughter was a high school sophomore, and our youngest was just entering sixth grade. We had lived in our previous house for ten years and it was really the only home they had ever known. My wife had also been heavily involved in the community and at school.

Since then, my family has flourished. But the decision to move for career growth—like many opportunities that came along—was born out of a place of adversity and uncertainty.

Three years before this time, I had left a very secure sales territory with Zimmer Orthopedics that I had successfully grown, earning five President Club honors in the process. I decided to run a distributorship for Biomet Orthopedics—something I had wanted to do for many years. It's interesting to note that these two Warsaw-based companies, who were then bitter rivals, have now merged. Even though my distributorship experienced rapid growth over those three years, I was suddenly faced with merging my distributorship with another adjacent and larger distributor. The parent company decided it could compete more effectively that way. I wasn't being forced to give up my distributorship but since they wanted to merge two states for their new model, it didn't make sense for me to continue independently.

I was again faced with a dilemma, this time internal. The management team that was put into place was not competent in my view. They didn't have the experience to know how to run a distributorship and it was evident from the beginning. I knew I would have to make a decision.

I automatically began to ask questions. "There has to be more out there for me, right?" I wanted to contribute, and I wanted to move my career to the next level in the process. Well, as you might have guessed, my questions continued to move me to the point where a decision had to be made. I prayed every day that I would make the right one. I knew those decisions would affect not only myself, but also those who were closest to me. These very same decisions had the potential to alter the destiny of my family forever.

Nothing will happen in your sales career —or in your life— until you take action.

By asking the best questions I knew how, I ultimately believe I made the right decision for us. Since that time my children have recognized dreams of their own, and things that once seemed so critical are but a distant memory. My oldest daughter, Lauren, is an RN with two children of her own. Our middle daughter, Stephanie, is now an attorney in Chattanooga, Tennessee. And our youngest daughter, Natalie, lives locally and works at a preschool.

My journey has brought me to three different positions over the last 13 years... each a step forward from the previous. While I don't know where this will all lead, I can tell you that I have a strong faith and that my dreams are turning into reality. I say "turning" rather than "turned" because the growth and learning process continue. There are constantly new and exciting things on the horizon.

Although it was difficult for my children to leave the security and fond memories behind, this new adventure brought us closer together. It made us all stronger and wiser. I believe this because it is the abundance of life experiences that most powerfully strengthens our character.

So don't be afraid to dream. Follow those dreams by asking yourself the questions that call you to action. Nothing will happen in your sales career—or in your life—until you take action.

You have everything to gain and a lot less to lose!

"Never give up, never slow down...and never ever die young."
~James Taylor

SUMMARY

- Everything you do or say in life will affect other people.

- Asking better questions is a call to action. It takes your dream from inside your mind, out of the bleachers, and onto the playing field.

- For any question you ask yourself, your brain will provide an answer... so it's imperative that you're asking the right questions.

- Follow your dreams by asking yourself those positively framed questions that call you to action.

CHAPTER 3

READY TO TAKE ACTION

Now that you understand what sales is, and that at the foundation are the Four Pillars, let's get ready to take action. I will introduce a process that you will be able to use in sales, life, communication, and relationships in general. By now you are beginning to develop a pretty good sense of where you are heading. Your house needs to be built on some pretty heavy-duty pillars—*honesty*, *integrity*, *knowledge*, and *genuine interest*—and it all sounds good, but there are obstacles at every turn.

The game of life isn't a walk in the park. So, before we launch into the process, let's talk about a few things, or at least bring to the surface those items that could get in your way.

PLAN FOR YOUR SUCCESS

How do you prepare to meet your day?

It's Sunday night and you have a huge day and a big week ahead. When is it time to prepare? I know it's been a busy weekend and you're both literally and metaphorically out of gas. You could probably just wait until the morning to fill up your tank, right? You could also wait to select your clothes until the morning and wait to make copies for that game-changing presentation or sales call.

But what do you think the successful salespeople are doing instead?

It would be a good bet that they filled up their gas tank on Sunday night, pressed their clothes, and laid out anything they needed for the next day, ready ahead of time.

I can tell you I have been both of these individuals. I can also tell you from experience that preparing the night before, and throwing procrastination out the window, will make all the difference for you. Hey, it's not easy to prepare for the coming week when you are just plain tired, but it will become the major difference in your quest for success rather than mediocrity.

> *"I demand more of myself than anyone else could ever expect."* ~Julius Irving

Let me ask you a question about those Sunday nights when you didn't prepare as well as you could have. Did you later go into that meeting, presentation, or sales call not as prepared as you would have liked?

Don't worry... I've done it, too. It's taken me years, but I can tell you now that I finally associate more pain with *not being prepared* than with getting prepared ahead of time.

For those of us in sales, preparation means all the work we put in behind the scenes—essentially everything we do in preparation that makes all the difference. No one will see the late nights reviewing a presentation, studying the competition, or making other sacrifices while you are locked in your office, but you will know that you are prepared because quietly you demanded excellence from yourself.

Some people have a gift in their chosen field or sport, but talent will only take you so far. Those who are naturally better in sales aren't always the most successful. Often, they don't ever develop that competitive nature and the biggest heart to become truly the best.

Tom Brady, the quarterback for the New England Patriots, was not selected until the sixth round of the 2000 draft—the 199th pick overall. Critics said he wouldn't play a year in the NFL. Twenty years and six Super Bowl rings later, they call him the G.O.A.T... the greatest of all time.

> **If you want more success, demand more from yourself than anyone else could possibly expect.**

Brady couldn't run as fast and didn't have the athletic build many quarterbacks had that year, but what he did have was a fierce determination. He prepared more, worked on his technique more, and as a result has a list of records and achievements that may never be broken in a lifetime. At the time of this writing, now 42 years old, Tom Brady is still winning and sometimes throwing the ball 60 yards down the field.

If you have the talent and are already good in sales, that's great. Chances are that you are doing a lot of what we are talking about here already, but whether you have an abundance of talent or not, there is no substitution for preparation. If you want the edge, if you want to become more successful than your competition or the colleagues in your company, demand more from yourself than anyone else could ever expect.

This will create the success habits that can't be broken. It doesn't mean you will never fail, but the times when you don't succeed will become less frequent. No valley will seem too low and no peak will ever be insurmountable. This is true because once you have experienced success you will know what to do, and you will have the answers that will get you back there. You will have earned the respect of your peers and they will begin to look to you as an example.

> *"A lot of times I find that people who are blessed with the most talent don't ever develop that attitude, and the ones who aren't blessed in that way are the most competitive and have the biggest heart."*
> *~Tom Brady*

THE POWER OF PURPOSE

Have you ever woken up in the morning and wished you had another hour or more of sleep? It seemed like you had only just closed your eyes, but it was already time to get up.

Who played this cruel trick on you? You probably had something to do that day that you really were not looking forward to. Maybe you had been telling yourself you were going to get up at 5:00 A.M. and go to the gym. You got your bag ready the night before and placed your sneakers by the bed. All you had to do was roll out of bed, put your sweats on, wash your face, and get in the car.

Yet when the alarm goes off, it's dark. That abrupt feeling of being startled takes over. You begin to have a conversation with yourself. (By the way, you're not crazy by talking to yourself. After all, no one else is up at that hour.) Somehow you hit snooze a few times, then finally roll out of bed at 6:00 A.M., too late to go to the gym before work. *That's okay*, you tell yourself. *I'll go this afternoon, or I'll go tomorrow.* You get the picture. If you're not careful, those mornings eventually turn into "Someday I'll..." and the *someday* never comes.

The opposite of this situation might occur if you're going on vacation or to a special event—something important you really want to do. You can't wait. In fact, who needs the alarm? You wake up before it even goes off. You jump out of bed and as you get ready, you're instantly thinking about what you're going to be doing that day.

I have found that when I really like what I'm doing and I have a plan, I am much more motivated to not only greet each new day, but I find I can't wait to get going. On the other hand, if I am less motivated because I don't like what I'm doing or there is something difficult about it, then I am going to prolong the inevitable just as long as possible... hitting the snooze button and staying in bed.

So how do you build a habit of being excited about greeting each new day? So much so that you spring out of bed with a passion for life and your career? To make that next sales call!

Purpose will get you out of bed every morning—the absolute conviction that you can make a difference in your life, and in so doing, you will have a positive influence on others, too.

"Good for you," you say, "but not for me." I beg to differ. If you are reading this, the two of us plus millions of other people have experienced very similar feelings. *The grass isn't always greener on the other side of the street*. Those folks are facing the same sorts of obstacles, trust me!

> **_Purpose_ will get you out of bed every morning.**

Anyone who has experienced real success in sales has faced major roadblocks somewhere along the way. I know that is a newsflash, but it is true. We may have struggled in different areas, but we have all faced things that seemed insurmountable at some point. The word "struggle" can sound harsh and will vary in degree from person to person, but it is there, and it implies challenges.

If you are not where you want to be, you don't need to accept it; but you do need to *acknowledge* it. If first, you acknowledge where you are and your current situation, you will be miles ahead of other people. If you recognize you are in a certain situation, a rut, a place you don't want to be in—maybe a relationship, a job, or a level in that job—then the power to acknowledge it and move on is important.

It is important because it is at this point that you get to *decide*. "Decide what?" you ask. You get to decide where you want to go from here.

"It's in our moments of decision that our destiny is shaped."
~Tony Robbins

You may sometimes recognize that there is an issue, but you may not want to act on it. Ostriches are notoriously good at this; they just stick their heads in the sand. Don't be an ostrich. Investigate or research what it is that needs to change, and then decide. Once you decide, the momentum of the process will lead you to action.

If you ever get a chance, watch the movie *Groundhog Day* with Bill Murray. It's a classic. Reporter Phil Collins is not happy with his life. He is a weatherman for a Philadelphia news station and is sent to Punxsutawney, Pennsylvania, with his crew to cover the groundhog and the ceremony where it sees or doesn't see its shadow, determining how many weeks of winter are left. Collins has obviously been down this road before and is unhappy with his current situation. He is not kind to his crew, or anyone for that matter. An approaching snowstorm holds him and the filming crew up overnight. Collins wakes the next morning to Sonny and Cher's "I Got You, Babe," but it's the same day as yesterday—Groundhog Day. You guessed it; Collins has to relive the day over and over again. Along the way he falls in love with a woman on his filming crew but by the end of each day he manages to kill the relationship. Slowly he makes little changes along the way—small but significant changes that alter the course of his life.

It's a struggle at first (there's that word again), but with every Groundhog Day he relives, people begin to slowly see the good in him as he learns to give back to the people of this small town. The culmination of who knows how many Groundhog Days ends at a dance where all the people he has touched along the way show their gratitude for what he has done for them. Phil has become a changed man and finally gets the girl. When he wakes up the next morning it's a brand new day, one with fresh new snow and blue skies.

You and I don't get to relive the same day, but sometimes we might wish we could, and other times we're just thankful that it's over.

We can't change the past Phil Collins did, but we can change the future and alter our destiny if we simply learn from the past. *Recognize* your current situation, *acknowledge* where you are, *investigate* to determine if you are satisfied with your current situation or if something needs to change, and finally *decide* whether or not you are happy with the way things are. If you are not, then begin to make small changes. Don't try to do it all at once. Make little consistent positive changes in your daily routine. When you do, those changes will become new habits. You will see the difference, and after you do, then make another small change, build on that previous one and so on.

Whether you work for yourself as an independent distributor or as a salesman for a major company, you hold the key to your future and your own destiny.

When you wake up each morning you have an opportunity. It's true that some mornings are easier than others, depending on what yesterday was like, but the most glorious thing about a new day is that it hasn't happened yet. You are staring at a blank canvas and at any moment you can choose the colors and the landscape of your new day.

A new day is a blank canvas. You get to choose the colors and the landscape.

Successful salespeople have an appreciation for yesterday because it provides lessons learned, but it doesn't trap them there. The lessons of yesterday hold the key to the successes of tomorrow.

When you wake up with this mindset, you wake closer to your goals and your dreams. You also have the opportunity to earn more; after all, that is part of your job.

The thing about yesterday is that you can't go back; you have no choice but to move forward.

"Discipline is the bridge between goals and accomplishment."
~Jim Rohn

SUMMARY

- Demand more from yourself than anyone would ever expect.

- Having a *purpose* will get you out of bed every morning.

- The lessons of yesterday hold the key to the success of tomorrow.

- You get to decide where you want to go from here.

CHAPTER 4

BELIEFS

Your beliefs dictate your activity. They will also get you through the fear. Whether something is true or not, the fact that you believe it to be true is all that matters. Humans are storytellers. We can come up with a story to validate anything we want, including why we should or shouldn't take specific actions, like making a cold call to a new customer or account.

When I was fresh out of the Marine Corps, I began my sales career working in my father's orthopedic distributorship. At that time there was little business for us in New Hampshire and Vermont, though I did an occasional trauma case to get my feet wet. I remember driving all the way to Keene, New Hampshire, to a doctor's office, but I could not even get out of the car. It was terrible. I was so afraid!

Afraid of what? I guess it was the unknown. I was 24 years old at the time and every surgeon seemed to be twice my age. I thought they were gods. What could I possibly sell to them? How could I talk intelligently about joint replacement? I had only seen a handful of surgeries.

I came up with every reason not to walk into that office. It was not my view of selling or whether someone else believed I was a good salesman. The problem was, I didn't believe in myself. I didn't believe in my abilities, and I didn't know enough about my product to have a strong belief that it was the best and that doctors should be using it and no one else's. In sales, this is what we know as "Call Reluctance."

Several years ago, when we still had cassette tapes, I picked up a program from a Tony Robbins late-night infomercial called "Personal Power." It was a 30-day program that I listened to over and over until I practically wore out the tape. Tony said the only reason for not taking action is associating more pain with that action than pleasure. A great example is someone who smokes—the person associates more pleasure from smoking than the risk to their health. They feel the pleasure of smoking in the moment, but the consequences are somewhere out there in the distant future, possibly lung cancer or dozens of other health related issues caused by the long-term effects of lighting up. It could be the same when a sales call is staring you in the face. You associate so much pain about what could happen and how that makes you feel that you don't follow through.

I believe success in sales, or in anything, comes from the belief that you can achieve what you set out to do.

The reality is, what you believe will determine your activities. As humans we create stories in our mind to validate actions we take and actions we fail to take. We have beliefs about everything from broader global convictions down to the minutest thing. If you believe people are good, then you will probably naturally give them the benefit of the doubt until they do something that proves otherwise. Conversely, if you believe "caveat emptor"—let the buyer beware—or hold a belief that salesmen are dishonest, then you will

Success comes from a belief in yourself.

definitely be on guard when purchasing your next car or appliance. Wouldn't that belief adversely affect your commitment to sales activities?

As children, these burgeoning beliefs are influenced by our parents, our surroundings, people we look up to or idolize, and events that become indelibly etched in our minds. You may never remember much about your early childhood years, however some of your beliefs will have been installed from a significant life event.

When I was about four years old, I almost drowned in a family friend's pool. It was a round above-ground pool and so you couldn't really see into it from a distance. I was with some other older kids and we had inner tubes that you could put your legs in. The other kids left the pool and I wanted to get out too, but when I tried, my inner tube tipped over and dumped me out. When I tried to stand up, the water was over my head and I couldn't make it to the side. All of a sudden, I heard my mother call my name from a distance. Out of instinct she came running to the pool and pulled me to safety. Over 50 years later I remember it like it was yesterday. To this day I fear pools and especially children around pools. Even though I now swim laps a few times a week and have become a good swimmer—and even though all of my children are now good swimmers, too—I was still overly cautious about them and their friends around water.

Events in our lives can either negatively affect us—leaving us shackled in chains that become more restrictive as we age—or positively affect us—becoming the lifeline we need to find the confidence to step forward into the unknown and try new things. The important thing to note is that factually it doesn't matter whether the event did or did not happen the way you remember. *It's whether you believe it to be true that makes all the difference.*

How do we relate this to sales?

It comes back to your view of selling, the sales profession, and the sales process. If you have a product you believe in, then you are more than halfway there because you have faith it will help your potential customer. Ask yourself these questions:

- Do you believe in your product or service?
- Do you believe you can help people with this product or service?
- Do you believe you are providing value by making people aware of this product or service?

If you believe these three things, then you will be able to face the obstacles that prevent others from making a sales call. I can't say that you won't still be nervous, but a strong belief will carry you through.

Take a good look at your product and go beyond its features and benefits. Why is it better than your competition? What need could it potentially fill? And how could it potentially help people? Armed with these answers, you can create a belief that becomes far reaching.

If you currently hold a negative view of selling, this understanding will help you shift that belief. Your sales success will soar when you understand you are providing a valuable service. It sometimes becomes complicated when you must make an appointment to get in front of that potential customer and find out whether they actually have a need for your product or service. If you answered yes to the three bullet points, you are well on your way.

Remember, what you believe makes all the difference. Your life is a story. It's your story, and the most incredible thing about it is that you get to write the next scene. And guess what... you have a lot of chapters left to compose in this novel called life!

BELIEF OF SELLING

When you believe in yourself and your abilities, and you believe in your product or service, and then combine your values with the Four Pillars of *honesty, integrity, knowledge,* and *genuine interest,* you will be able to develop a strong commitment to action on a daily basis.

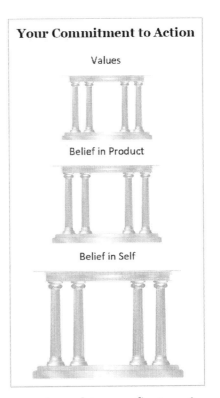

Why does selling get such a bad rap from so many people anyway? Why are we always on guard as customers when we go to make a purchase? Why is it such a chore? (Not for everyone, of course, because some people see it as a challenge, or a quest to get the best deal.)

What's the first thing you did when you bought your first car? Chances are you at least showed it off a little. I drove to my parents and gave my dad and fiancée a ride. It was a grey 1985 Ford Mustang. I loved that car! But auto purchases are not easy if you don't have a salesperson who really connects with you and tries to understand your needs.

Back in the mid-1980s, when I sold cars at Forest City Chevrolet in Portland, Maine, a crusty old used car salesman named Sterling Boyington told me, "It's not the deal you get. It's the deal you think you get." In his mid-50s, Sterling appeared to know everyone in Portland. He would outsell the other 10-15 salesmen just about every month and win more Salesman of the Month plaques than anyone.

He believed he was helping his customers and doing them a service by finding them the right car. He was relentless and would talk to anyone, looking past the rejection other car salesmen got every day, because he didn't take negative attitudes personally. He never got mired down in the fear of rejection or what anyone else thought about him. He was comfortable with himself, and others could see his confidence.

This man stood 5'7" and weighed only 150 pounds soaking wet, but he walked with giants. He loved selling cars and helping his customers. Anything else that may have kept him from accomplishing that task was secondary. He later started his own used car company and was very successful.

It's funny how we try to overcomplicate things. This used car salesman made selling a very simple process, and I believe he did that with most everything in his life. He believed in himself, and his abilities. He also believed he was providing a great service for his customers. Those who didn't become his customers lost an opportunity, at least in his mind. He never overcomplicated life. "This business is simple," he said. "You got a product, you got a price, and you got a deal or you don't."

One of my sales directors today reminds me a lot of Sterling—committed 100% to the activities that will grow his business. He believes in his product, the company, his abilities, and he will speak to anyone. He is a challenge to manage on any given day, but with his overall belief in product, abilities, and his belief in selling, he is unstoppable.

Whatever type of sales you are involved in, from orthopedics to used cars, the principles remain the same. If you believe in yourself and your abilities, if you believe in your product and that it is of value to your potential customers, then your belief in selling will also be aligned.

If your car has ever been out of alignment, you notice because it does not want to follow a straight track down the road, and instead wanders either to the left or the right. Aligning your beliefs is just as important as aligning the wheels of your car. When all the factors that influence your belief in selling are in alignment, you will become unstoppable as you navigate your path to success in sales.

BELIEF IN YOUR PRODUCT

When others speak about a good salesman, I've often heard the phrase, "He could sell ice to Eskimos." I guess you could interpret that a couple of different ways. Maybe the Eskimos don't need more ice because, after all, they already live in a world of snow and ice—and selling them more would be selling them something they don't need.

> **If you believe in yourself and your product, then your belief in selling will also be aligned.**

Most would view trying to sell ice to Eskimos as not having the customer's best interests in mind. However, if buying ice in premade blocks could allow the Eskimos to build their igloos quicker, maybe they could spend more time fishing for whales. In this case, wouldn't you be helping the customer by actually doing something for and with him? That Eskimo could skip the hours cutting and shaping blocks to make his igloo and instead spend the time fishing and potentially providing food and resources for his family and the village.

When your customer's needs come first, you can feel good about selling, and then later witnessing the results it makes in your customer's life.

While conducting a sales training several years ago I asked a group of orthopedic sales reps how they felt about being seen or viewed as a salesman. To my own amazement none of them wanted that label associated with them. Instead they were attaching other words to describe what they did, such as "Consultant" or "Representative," leaving "Sales" out of the title.

I've experienced the same thing in business after business when someone hands me their card without the word "sales" attached. It's as if they're saying, "See? I'm not one of those terrible sales people here to take your money. No, not me. I'm here to help." But the bottom line is that people still know why you are there. It's not the label "salesman" that is going to make your prospects turn and run, though. It's what you believe and what you do as a person that will ultimately make the difference.

If you believe in your product or service, if you believe you are helping someone, or that your product or service will provide a benefit to someone, then you should be proud to represent it. Sure, you are going to meet rejection and that can be scary, but just think about the bigger picture and the service you are providing when you introduce a product or service to those who need it. Don't worry, customers will be able to tell quickly whether or not you are genuinely interested in them and whether you have their best interests in mind.

It's what you—and only you—believe that matters. This will change how you view your position as a salesperson and will dictate the activities you undertake in order to become successful. Those same beliefs will dictate whether or not you spring into action every day.

You might ask yourself, "How can I sell against major competitors that have been doing it much longer and may even have more resources than me or my company?"

The answer I found is through what I have done thousands of times over. I looked for a unique story to tell. I spoke with customers who used the product—in my industry it's the surgeons who designed the knee and hip systems—and I researched the technology. I observed the surgical cases and I spoke with surgeons who had put in several hundred implants with good results. I built my belief in the product first, and without fail I could then confidently tell the story about it and the benefits it would have for their patients.

Honesty, integrity, knowledge, and *genuine interest...* If you are honest with yourself and others, if you stay true to your values, your abilities, and know your product and the competition's better... *and* you believe in yourself and your product... you will commit to the activities that drive you to success in sales, as well as all areas of your life.

> *"What the mind of man can conceive and believe, it can achieve." ~Napoleon Hill*

SUMMARY

- It's what you believe that matters, and what you believe that will make all the difference.

- The events in our lives can both negatively affect us—leaving us shackled in chains that become more restrictive as we age—or positively affect us—becoming the lifeline we need to find the confidence to step forward into the unknown and try new things.

- When your customer's needs come first, you can feel good about selling, witnessing the results it makes in your customer's life.

Long-term relationships built on the Four Pillars of *honesty, integrity, knowledge,* and *genuine interest* will stand the test of time.

> *"Commitment is what transforms a promise into reality."* ~Abraham Lincoln

CHAPTER 5

PREPARATION

You can strengthen your belief in your abilities every day. What you believe can either become the chains that shackle you to limiting beliefs or they can become the ladder you climb to new and greater heights.

VISUALIZATION

In his program "Psychology of Winning," Denis Waitley speaks about an Air Force Colonel, a pilot who had been shot down during the Vietnam War and spent several years in confinement at the famed "Hanoi Hilton," a prison camp. He talks about how the colonel, who was an avid golfer, played his favorite course every day in his mind. He walked every fairway, made every putt, and replaced every divot. Upon finally returning home but without having picked up a club in years, the colonel played his best round of golf.

This is an amazing benefit of the power of visualization.

I have been involved with horses for a long time but hadn't competed in over five years. I recently started competing again in the hunter/jumper ring after the long layoff. Even though my travel schedule kept me away for days at a time, I trained fairly regularly. When a non-rated show was held just an hour from our farm, I decided to jump back in, so to speak.

A friend was showing in a different class early in the morning and then I had to wait until the end of the day before my horse and I went into the ring. There were a series of eight fences which would be jumped in a designed sequence three different times. Each time you enter the ring to jump the eight fences it's called a "trip." The good thing for me that day was that I got to see the sequence—the order that the horse would follow to jump around the course. For a few hours off and on, I watched other horses compete, and then I began to visualize each jump, each turn, and each line of fences.

In my mind, I saw myself going deep into the corner to give my horse the best approach possible. I could count the strides between each fence and look for the next one up ahead as I would turn a corner. I could already feel the pace, see the spot where my horse would be leaving the ground on each approach, and feel the rhythm as the horse would canter down the line.

That afternoon my horse was the second in the ring. Our approach to the first jump was not our greatest, but after that, it was almost perfect. The other two trips into the ring that day were beautiful. I saw a video of the last trip and another trainer could be heard breaking conversation to say, "Watch this. It's pretty," to which the other person replied, "It really is."

My horse and I won all three trips that day and took the championship in that particular class over fences. The feeling after such a long absence was tremendous, a high I want to remember.

Aside from having a very good horse who knew his job well, my visualization of the course over and over in my head made all the difference. It was almost like I had been there before when I had actually never been in that ring.

I used visualization that day because of the story I have heard countless times about how athletes use it in competitions. I employed this technique because I wanted to win. Because of this visualization, I performed at a higher level. In my mind's eye I had ridden that course several times.

Remember those words of Napoleon Hill, "What the mind can conceive, the body can achieve." My mother's version was, "You can do anything you put your mind to." She and Napoleon Hill were both right. I know you can achieve your dreams as well if you just visualize it and see it in your mind's eye.

If you really want to be successful in sales, recognize and then acknowledge where you are in your life and your career. Investigate, become your own personal detective, and deep down decide if you are okay where you are or if you have the desire and the absolute need to make a change. If a change is an absolute must, then plot out the things you will need to do to get there. Begin to take action steps that will move you forward. Visualize where you see yourself in the future. See it all first in your mind's eye and the actions will come naturally.

To take that one step further, you can say the visualization is your practice, and your trial run.

At every sales training I have ever attended, when the phrase 'role-play' is mentioned, I can feel the energy leave the room. Talk about the wind being taken from your sails! No one likes to do it because it's uncomfortable, especially in front of peers. Role-playing is awkward but in your mind's eye visualization can put you there in that next sales call as if it was happening now.

Let's next take this preparation beyond the classroom and break it down even further. When you visualize your success, what does that look like to you? What first impression will you make on your customer?

DRESS THE PART

When people talk about *dressing for success*, what do they mean? Begin by seeing yourself as a success in your business. If you could watch yourself making the perfect sales call, what would it look like?

What if you could take a step back and run the video of that same situation? Visualize how you would be dressed. Would you look professional? Would your shoulders be back exuding confidence? Would you speak with conviction? Can you see yourself there? Would you look people in the eye instead of glancing away when you spoke? Would you listen to really understand the person you are speaking with?

If you visualize all this in your mind's eye now, and make it so vivid that you find yourself even mouthing the words you might say, then you are further along in my estimate than 90% of your peers walking into a similar call.

I agree that role-playing in a classroom environment with your peers is not easy but you will always find trainers who want to include it once they have given you all the product information you can digest. The assumption is that you need to practice how you would use this new knowledge in a sales call. It's all with good intentions and sometimes you just have to grin and bear it, hearing my mom's words again... "Anything you learn is not lost."

People make judgments about you within 7 seconds.

Consider your dress as part of your daily preparation, looking the part of the successful sales representative, walking like you would if you had already achieved your quota, speaking not arrogantly but confidently as if prepared and *knowledgeable*, and listening with *genuine interest* to what people have to say.

There is no guarantee you will make the perfect call but with preparation, you will have put yourself into a much better position for success than the majority of your competition.

SEVEN SECONDS

As much as you can possibly prepare, you'll never get a second chance to make a first impression. People make judgments about you within seven seconds after they first lay eyes on you. That's right... seven seconds! This doesn't give us a lot of time. Just a second shorter than a successful bull ride.

Years ago there was a standard uniform of sorts for the sales professional. For the man it was a blue blazer or sport coat, coupled with khaki or gray pants. For the woman it was a conservative dress in a solid color and heels.

Have we moved beyond that in today's world?

When I first began my sales career in the '80s, Fridays were usually a casual day and people could dress down in jeans, but on the first four days of the week it was more formal. Today many companies are business casual except for major meetings where both customers, company personnel, and sales representatives wear formal attire.

My opinion is to try and look my best at all times. But then again, I'm a Marine and I will always have that internal military discipline. My father served in the Air Force back in the '50s and told me about the "gig line." Essentially, for a man, your left edge of your belt should be in line with the edge of your shirt seam and it's what I still do every day. When I'm traveling, I won't leave my hotel room unless my shirt is pressed and my shoes are polished. I even pack a small steaming iron that is great for taking wrinkles out of sport coats and suit coats that have been packed away. I'm sure it would work equally well for dresses and blouses.

These are just my opinions and you should dress to the level of your own comfort. First impressions are important, and part of that seven seconds comes from your attire and, I believe, your overall persona—the confidence you exude and how you project yourself. Dressing well makes you feel good, and for me that always gives me a little extra boost of confidence that reminds me, "You got this. You're prepared."

If you are attending a meeting and the memo says business casual, then dress business casual. Don't overdress. But if it's more formal and you know it, never dress down.

However you choose to dress, do it in a tasteful way that makes you feel good about yourself and equally gives you the opportunity to make a good initial impression, especially if it is a first-time meeting with a customer.

How you prepare will:

- Play a large role in making the best first impression.

- Let your customer know you're serious about wanting to do business with them.

- Show your respect for those you're meeting by being dressed as a professional, ready to do business.

The next time you make a sales call, do more than just prepare. Dress in a way that gives you the opportunity to make a good impression before you even speak your first words. You could do all the planning in the world, and do all the right things—analyze the situation, put all the right literature together, know your client's personality—yet walk in and not have a chance if you're not dressed appropriately.

When you plan your next sales call, factor in how you will look to the customer and how others will perceive you. Even more important, use it as your own tool to give you that extra boost of confidence.

ORGANIZATION

What does the word *organization* mean to you in terms of preparation? Do you lead an organized life, neat as a pin, with nothing out of place? Or is your life an organized chaos? Do you go in cycles or brief spurts? You may reach a point of frustration where you say, "I'm mad as hell and I'm not going to take it anymore," and then finally you spring into action and purge all the stuff that's cluttering your desk.

If you are super organized in your life, I applaud you. I have three daughters and they are all different. The youngest, Natalie, is creative. She writes music, shares my love for horses, and is always the last one out the door. Her room was always a mess and usually took the help of her sisters to get it cleaned up. My middle daughter, Stephanie, is an attorney now in Tennessee. She always had unbelievable organizational skills growing up and all through school. When we were going on a trip, she had all her things staged by the door without fail every time. Our oldest daughter Lauren, now a Registered Nurse, was somewhere in between. She possessed good organizational skills, was always determined and could be very creative at times.

I remember one evening when I was helping Natalie with Government homework. The assignment was on the federalist papers, something I hadn't seen in years. Since my middle daughter had the same teacher, I decided to call Stephanie who was a freshman in college to see if she could help. When I told her what chapter and assignment Natalie was on, she calmly said, "Dad, go up to my room and look in my closet. The third binder from the left on the top shelf is my government binder."

When I retrieved it, I couldn't believe what I found. It had all her notes for every chapter, all in order and in a way that could help Natalie get through her assignment. I was so impressed by the level of Stephanie's organization—even as a child. I have often wished a little of that skill would rub off on me.

In business just as in daily life, a certain level of organizational preparation is required to keep you moving forward.

A friend who shares a love for horses, with three of her own, has tremendous organizational skills. An engineer by education, she has been in the sales side of the energy industry for several years. I had wondered if she would do well when she got into sales. I shouldn't have worried.

Her philosophy is, "As far as preparation, develop a system, and do that same thing every day. That way when you are in a time crunch it is automatic." This is another way of creating positive rituals that will not only keep you organized but make you more efficient.

There is a recurring theme in this book, and it may be over simplified, but it is a key to success in anything you do. You must first want something bad enough that you become persistent in all the activities that move you toward it. Some people develop these organizational skills at a young age; others get mad as hell and just won't take it anymore, so they force themselves to change. They do what's necessary because they see the brightness of the future. Consequently, they don't like the alternative.

When you're on your way to achieving the level of success you desire, developing a system that works for you will be foundational. It won't take long before consistent daily action becomes a habit.

You just need to decide. You can read books on organization, or ask other people what they do, or try to forge your own path. It's important to keep trying different things until you become the best version of you.

Maybe organization isn't a struggle for you at all, but if it is, remember that the journey of a thousand miles begins with one step. Sometimes we get caught up in life and dig ourselves into a rut we later can't seem to get out of. Those of you in the North know what it's like to be stuck in the mud or a snowbank with your car. The more you rock back and forth, the deeper the rut. You just spin and spin, right in sync with the definition of insanity—doing the same thing over and over again expecting a different result.

In your daily activities, how often have you found yourself just going through the motions, feeling you're busy but never seeming to move things ahead? With regard to sales, you may feel you're doing a lot of things, but not gaining any ground. Sometimes you are so busy you don't take time for yourself, or your family.

TIME MANAGEMENT

In the timeless reference book, *The 7 Habits of Highly Effective People,* Stephen Covey introduced the four quadrants of the Time Management Matrix. Through a series of questions, this matrix helps you map where you are spending most of your time. It is valuable to understand that where you spend your time and the degree that you spend in certain quadrants can have a profound effect on your daily activities. It can also reveal if you are spending enough time on self-renewal.

These four quadrants include tasks which are both (I) Urgent and Important, (II) Not Urgent but Important, (III) Urgent but Not Important, and (IV) Not Urgent and Not Important. Unfortunately, most of us spend way too much time dealing with tasks in the latter two quadrants because they are less daunting.

Let's take a look at how this matrix can be adapted for sales-people.

	Urgent	Not Urgent
Important	• Prospect meetings **I** • Client follow-up • Forecast deadlines • Product issues • Request for Proposals (RFPs)	• Presentation prep **II** • Product knowledge • Sales call planning • Relationship building • Advancement Seminars
Not Important	• Interruptions, **III** some phone calls • Text messages & emails • Water cooler conversations • Putting out fires	• Social media **IV** • Busywork • Web browsing • TV • Sales "milk runs"

Figure 1: Adaptation of Stephen Covey's
Time Management Matrix[1] as related to sales

---

[1] Covey, Stephen. *The 7 Habits of Highly Effective People: Powerful Lessons in Personal Change.* Free Press, 2004.

Sales Quadrant I

We can't avoid Quadrant I activity because it involves daily work activities that must be dealt with, including projects, meetings, deadlines, and crises that catch us off guard. **Quadrant I activities are both urgent and important**. The danger is that these can turn into a never ending circle.

When you spend so much time in Quadrant I that you get burned out, you drift into Quadrant III. The phone calls and interruptions make it difficult to stay on task. Even more distressing is that those activities you will naturally fall prey to in **Quadrant III are not important but they are urgent.**

Sales Quadrant III

Many people spend most of their time in Quadrants I, III, and IV. When the urgent and important Quadrant I activities end up pushing you to drift into the urgent but unimportant activities of Quadrant III, you get a false sense of accomplishment and productivity because you are filling your day with busy work. And you will definitely be tired at the end of a day. You'll be so tired and mentally drained that it keeps you from the Quadrant I deadlines and then you drift away into Quadrant IV.

Sales Quadrant IV

Quadrant IV can best be described as those activities that allow you to escape. **Quadrant IV tasks are neither urgent nor important.** They consist entirely of busy work, too much TV, and those time-wasting activities that do nothing to help you revitalize yourself. Too much time in this quadrant can be very harmful. Without time for self-renewal, it can eventually lead to an unhappy state of mind, poor performance, and dreams that begin to die instead of flourish.

So how do we avoid the spiral? How do we get out of the weeds and the woods? We can sharpen the saw, of course!

Sales Quadrant II

Covey's Quadrant II contains tasks that become habit. It is the quadrant of self-renewal. The woodsman's tale illustrates this perfectly, in which a man is cutting down a tree. After a few hours, his saw gets dull, but he ignores advice to take a 15-minute break to sharpen it. The man claims he is too busy to stop, so it takes him another several hours to finish the job. The moral is that if he had only taken a quick break, he could've saved hours in the long run.

And what sharpens the saw? This consists of doing the activities that rejuvenate your body and soul: taking the time for planning and preparation, uncovering your individual mission, developing your goals, and understanding what you value most.

Unfortunately the reason we spend little time here is because **although Quadrant II activities are important, they are not urgent!** The underlying principles of Quadrant II activities allow us to do everything just mentioned so that we can make Quadrant I decisions and perform at a high level.

We must learn to prioritize, and even say "No" sometimes. Time well spent in Quadrant II allows us to spend less time in Quadrant III, and virtually no time in Quadrant IV where we often get caught up in the "thick of thin things." It helps us get a firm handle on the rudder and steer our ships into the wind. In Quadrant II we get to spend time with our families, we get to contribute, we get to learn, and we get to renew our spirit so that we move forward with conviction.

When we arrive back in Quadrant I afterward, we make better decisions. No one ever dies saying they wished they had spent more time at the office, however how many of us wished we had spent more special moments with our families and the people and hobbies we value most.

If you haven't read *The 7 Habits of Highly Effective People*, it's still in print after 30 years since its first publication in 1989. I often refer back to it to remind myself how important the planning and preparation of Quadrant II really is.

The Time Management Matrix is fourth-generation planning. It is not simple To Do lists where your schedule manages you; it is so much more. It is a commitment to prioritizing the activities of planning, preparation, mission, and values, so that you not only perform at a higher level, but you enjoy the process.

To clearly illustrate the power of organizing and prioritizing to optimize your time and talents, watch Stephen Covey's four-minute "Big Rocks" lesson[2] (see Figure 2).

Figure 2: Stephen Covey's "Big Rocks" presentation, available on YouTube.

---

[2] https://resources.franklincovey.com/the-8th-habit/bigrocks

SUMMARY

- Visualize where you see yourself in your mind's eye. Then practice role-playing your sales calls and other important activities. Map out your strongest responses and replay the visualization until the actions come naturally.

- You never get a second chance to make a first impression. People make judgments about you within seven seconds after they first lay eyes on you. When you make a positive first impression, everything that follows becomes easier.

- There is no substitute for preparation. Like Julius Irving, demand more from yourself than anyone else could ever expect.

- Develop an organizational system that works for you. It doesn't take long before consistent action on a daily basis becomes a habit. You will never be able to avoid the urgent and important Quadrant I activities, but by sharpening the saw, you will become far more efficient.

CHAPTER 6

THE POWER OF PURPOSE

When John McCain, the former U.S. Senator from Arizona, passed away from a brain tumor at age 81, many had forgotten his earlier history. They didn't even know what this man had endured in his life yet still managed to become extremely successful. In death, McCain transcended labels of political party and instead ascended to a place etched in the public's heart for eternity.

So why is this relevant to sales? McCain came from a military family and his father and grandfather were admirals and naval academy graduates just as he was. In October 1967, John McCain was shot down over Hanoi in North Vietnam during the Vietnam War. He spent five and a half years in confinement under terrible conditions and endured horrendous beatings. He was severely injured during the crash of his fighter jet and you might wonder how he survived at all.

> With *purpose* and *dedication*, you become unstoppable.

Upon finally returning home, John McCain could have had the most inconsequential conclusion to his life and an end to his story. He could have given up, packed it in, and said, "That's it. I've done enough," but here is the point. Instead he summoned the greatness that I believe all of us possess... but few tap into.

Denis Waitley said, "Through complacency comes the lull of apathy but through adversity comes the call to greatness." John McCain answered that call. He answered through a life of service and dedication. His sense of purpose stemmed from a deep love of his country and a desire to give back.

Purpose, dedication, service... if you can find that purpose for yourself, if you can dedicate deeply to that purpose—so deeply that you become unstoppable—then you will relentlessly pursue your dreams, and see clearly your vision. Then you too can make a difference in your own life and the lives of others.

Making a positive impact on others and making a difference in their lives is a way of giving back. Remember, you have an effect on everyone you speak with or come into contact with on a daily basis. You hold the key to whether that experience will have a positive or negative impact.

"Today is only one day in all the days that will ever be. But what will happen in all the other days that ever come can depend on what you do today."

~Ernest Hemingway, For Whom the Bell Tolls

If you are that person who is driven, you will touch many people over the course of your life. You have the power to make a difference—a positive difference—and a positive impact. On your road to success in life and in sales, whatever that is for you, wouldn't it be a great feeling to know that you made a positive difference and lifted others along the way?

With people, just as in math, the whole is equal to the sum of its parts. It is purpose that drives us. Our purpose is the fuel that sets our cause into motion. When you find your purpose, become dedicated to your cause, and serve others along the way, in turn the people whose lives you touch will view you with respect, and you will not only have made a positive difference in your life, but in theirs, too.

A PERSON'S NAME IS THE SWEETEST SOUND

Dale Carnegie said in his timeless book, *How to Win Friends and Influence People*, "A person's name to that person is the sweetest and most important sound in any language." When speaking with someone, we should use their name often at the appropriate times. The person will feel you are engaged, and the repetition will ensure you have a much better chance at remembering that person's name.

I have been guilty of drawing a blank from time to time, especially if I see someone I haven't spoken to for a long while. It can be embarrassing, especially when your brain is spending time trying to remember a name and you wind up missing details in the new conversation.

There are various methods for learning and remembering people's names. Dale Carnegie's method is called the LIRA formula.[3] This simple acronym can help you, too.

1. **L**ook and Listen

   Focus on the person speaking and understand clearly what their name is.

2. **I**mpression

   Remember what the person looks like, including physical features or the surroundings in which you met.

3. **R**epetition

   Repeat the person's name in conversation as appropriate. Then repeat it in your head as much as possible to solidify.

4. **A**ssociation

   Associate similar words or landmarks to help anchor the name in your memory.

---

3 http://dalecarnegieboston.tumblr.com/post/26913630460/dale-tip-6-a-persons-name-is-the-sweetest

After using this technique, remembering names will become much easier. Practice it with everyone you interact with, and make it a habit. When you apply this formula, you'll see quick success, and it will help you forge stronger relationships instantly.

Whatever method you use, just being more mindful and actually listening to what someone is saying will help you form a lasting impression and will help you remember their name as well as details about them. Then the act of remembering something about that person later—even if you haven't seen them in a while—will also solidify the respect they feel for you because you took the time to remember them.

Let's face it, nothing happens in this world unless we are able to communicate—and not just communicate, but communicate effectively. In the years before cell phones, texting, Facetime, Skype, Slack, webinars, Facebook, or Instagram, we had to actually speak with people one on one. Have you ever sent a text message that someone misinterpreted? At best, it leads to more text messages and even a phone call to explain what was trying to be said in the original message. But at worst it can foster unhealthy future communication with that person.

Don't just communicate... communicate *effectively.*

It's a vicious circle. Our society has changed rapidly and with technological advancements continuing at a feverish pace, changes in the way we communicate will continue. I don't mean to imply that they are all negative. Just recently, two of my sisters went to Sicily to visit the place where our grandparents came from. For ten days I received beautiful pictures via text messages and phone calls which were free through Facebook Messenger. Twenty years ago I would have had to wait until they returned home to see those pictures, or maybe I would have received an expensive phone call if I were lucky. Instead, it was a great feeling to hear about their journey as it was happening. It was almost like I was with them on their travels.

The danger of such advancements in communication is that we come to rely upon them so heavily that we lose the personal touch. This can lead directly to messages being misinterpreted. In business and sales, we need to communicate fast and effectively in order to keep up. You must use and appreciate the abundance of media and platforms for staying in touch.

You may text on a daily basis, and email daily, but I also like to call people. I like to hear the sound of their voice—because the inflection can tell you instantly whether they are having a good day or a bad day, or if they are genuinely excited or even upset about something.

This enhanced knowledge helps me appreciate much more about what is going on at that moment in their life. The next time you consider sending a text that is equivalent to *War and Peace...* ask yourself if this person would benefit more from hearing the sound of your voice as opposed to reading a long text? How much longer would it really take to say, "Hello, how are you? I got your text but wanted to hear a little more about what was on your mind. Is now a good time to talk?"

I recently saw a very touching segment on the TV series *America's Got Talent*. A young lady came to the stage with a ukulele and in the audience stood her interpreter. You see, this 23-year-old-woman had lost her hearing due to a connective tissue disease while in a music program in college. She had given up on music because she became legally deaf and could no longer hear. At one point she told her father while driving one day, "Dad, I can't remember what your voice sounds like anymore."

It is unbelievably sad that any of our God-given gifts can be taken away. It almost seems cruel to have experienced the gift of sound or sight and then lose it. Can you imagine how that must feel?

However, this exceptional young woman never gave up. She memorized scales and used vibration to follow the flow of the music. Her voice is beautiful. She is now following her dream again. She could have given up multiple times, or could have become complacent and apathetic, but instead she rose to the challenge.[4] Through her adversity she heard the words clearly inside and answered the call to greatness.

There are several important points here but the first is that communication is essential in our lives. Sometimes we take for granted that we have the option to hear the sound of someone else's voice. Instead we replace it with all the technology and social media apps available to us. But imagine if you could no longer hear the voice of a parent, a friend, a spouse, a girlfriend or boyfriend, a brother or sister. How would that make you feel?

I'm not trying to depress you, but what I am trying to point out is that your voice may be important to someone, too. If you can find the time today, think twice before sending that long text message. Instead, use your fingers to dial the number and hear that person's voice. It could make all the difference in your day... and theirs.

YOUR PERSONALITY DETERMINES YOUR STYLE OF COMMUNICATION

Have you ever tried to communicate with someone you found overbearing? You couldn't get a word in. Every time you tried to speak, they either filled in the blanks for you or spoke over top of you. Then they went on with their thought.

How did this make you feel? Did you feel as though the person really cared about you or what you had to say? Did you feel like they respected you or your opinion or had *genuine interest* in you? My guess is probably not.

---

[4] Watch Mandy Harvey's stunning performance and hear her story at https://youtu.be/oHUuCLgfMpo

Could you be that person?

Or do you often find it's difficult to speak to a person who is naturally more reserved than you? They would rather listen and hear what you have to say and they don't comment much because they are taking it all in and processing.

How about a conversation with someone who can't seem to stay on the subject? This person is fun to be around but would rather talk about what they did on the weekend as opposed to getting down to the task at hand.

> **Your personality style dictates the way you communicate and the way you receive information.**

Your personality style dictates the way you communicate and the way you receive information. It is part of who you are. People you know will come to understand you and communicate with you naturally based on these traits.

We are all created as individuals and the greatest thing is that as individuals, we are all different. But being different and having our own personality style and our own style of communication doesn't make us any more or less better than the next person. It simply dictates how we prefer to communicate.

I heard a comment recently that understanding personality styles allows us to play in the same sandbox together. While this person was essentially correct, there is obviously so much more to it. Understanding our personality style and behavioral traits can tell us a lot about who we are and how we communicate. But more important, it can inform us about our colleagues and our customers and potential customers.

After completing this book, you will not only be able to use personality and behavioral trait information in the sales process, but also when communicating with anyone. When I was studying for my MBA, we often worked in teams and groups. On a New Venture project—creating everything that would go into a startup company—there were four of us in the group, each with a different personality style. Two of the individuals were very analytical. One was supportive with an analytical side, and the other was me, more driven than analytical.

I was chosen by the team because they wanted someone with sales experience. You may already begin to see that there were probably going to be clashes here and there. Looking back, the most rewarding thing about this project was not the project itself but rather the lessons in interpersonal relationships.

Here were four people from different backgrounds, world views, and personality styles, however we learned to collaborate without kicking sand at each other and became very close.

I worked most closely with the woman who was the supportive analytical member. Our world views couldn't have been further apart. She spoke slower and more methodically than I did. She was highly organized but we both recognized the difference in our communication style. One evening she came to my house to work on a poster for our project. We had a tremendous amount of fun putting it together and it came out fantastic—or at least we thought so. Despite our initial differences, I came to realize she was a great person and I am happy to say we are still friends today.

Understanding personality traits allows you to find common ground

Understanding one's personality and behavioral traits allows you to find the common ground needed to build relationships. Such strong relationships are built on trust, and in a sales environment, you can't expect to have loyalty or long-term customers without it.

In the next chapter we will begin to discuss different personality styles so you can communicate more effectively... understanding your own style and quickly assessing that of the person you are speaking with.

SUMMARY

- You have an effect—either positive or negative—on everyone you speak with or come into contact with on a daily basis.

- When speaking with someone (especially someone new), you should use the person's name frequently during a conversation at the appropriate times.

- Being different and having your own personality and communication style doesn't make you any more or less better than the next person. It just dictates how you prefer to communicate.

- Understanding one's personality and behavioral traits allows you to find the common ground needed to build relationships.

PART TWO

The Personality Styles

CHAPTER 7

UNDERSTANDING PERSONALITY STYLES

There are several companies that market personality style assessments. Some refer to them as "personality styles," some use the term "social style," while still others incorporate a deeper behavioral style assessment that integrates behavioral traits, a primary personality style, and adaptive styles that you may possess. Myers Briggs, Gallop, Insights, Social Styles, and Personalysis are just a few. All of these are primarily built on the work of Carl Jung who was influential in the fields of psychiatry, anthropology, archaeology, literature, philosophy, and religious studies.

In this chapter I introduce my own assessment tool that is short, yet quickly allows you to evaluate a person's style during conversation, without the need for lengthy or expensive testing. While it is not scientific, it is based on 30 years of interaction in a sales environment. This will not only help you during sales calls but also during *any* conversation. If you understand your own style and then learn best how to communicate with people in their preferred way, you will find yourself effectively communicating with everyone you meet. You will also learn more about the people you interact with... and yourself at the same time.

This skill helps you not only during sales calls... but during *any* conversation.

Before we talk about individual personality styles, review the assessment on the following page. Take a few minutes to circle your answers, then tally up the results.

SALES PERSONALITY ASSESSMENT

**Answer without spending too much time on any one question.
Circle your first instinct.**

How do you most closely describe your personality:

- a) outgoing, engaging, people-oriented
- b) direct, dominant in conversation
- c) cooperative, affable; relationships are important
- d) analytical; situations are often black and white with no in-between

Which of these best reflects your manner of speech:

- a) lots of energy and inflection, enthusiastic
- b) deliberate and intentional, not animated unless agitated
- c) pleasant and easy-going, affable, caring
- d) slow and reserved, but confident

In conversation, you are:

- a) upbeat
- b) to the point, brief
- c) a good listener
- d) inquisitive

Your posture and stance are most often:

- a) open and inviting
- b) straight and sometimes rigid
- c) dependent upon the situation
- d) reserved

Which of these best describes your office:

- a) cluttered but welcoming
- b) awards and recognition photos displayed
- c) neat with family photos and keepsakes displayed
- d) utterly organized, even a bit sterile

Your preferred working pace is:

a) go with the flow
b) fast and decisive
c) slow and steady
d) calculated yet efficient

In committees, your decision-making process is:

a) likely to go with popular vote
b) decisive, not second-guessing
c) preferring to please everyone
d) determined by facts and figures

On an average day, your schedule:

a) often runs overtime due to off-topic conversations
b) tries to fit too much in
c) is leisurely paced
d) runs according to plan

Your business dress code can best be described as:

a) casual, sometimes disheveled
b) formal, well-groomed
c) neat, but not necessarily the latest fashion
d) conservative

Frequent gestures or actions include:

a) talking with your hands, animated
b) pacing, looking at the clock
c) measured, or dependent on the situation
d) arms folded, perhaps glasses perched on end of nose

SALES PERSONALITY ASSESSMENT SCORING

Add up the number of answers for each letter choice and fill in the total below. This assessment is not scientific but will quickly give you the information required to assess your own and your customer's styles. When you understand how theirs relates to yours, you will be able to optimize the time in the sales call that will help to build a long lasting relationship much sooner.

TOTAL

a) __4__ Enthusiast
b) __1__ Dominator
c) __2__ Moderator
d) __3__ Analyst

The two opposites?

The highest two results are your dominant styles. Keep in mind that these may adapt from a work environment to your home or personal environment. For instance, you may be more dominant at work yet more of an enthusiast at home. We all tend to have an adaptive style. I have found that in my work environment I meet what I perceive as necessary for me to function at a high level in my role. At home I tend to go with the flow.

Depending on how you adapt and how closely your natural style is to your work environment, you may find that it requires much more energy to function at the level you perceive as necessary to be successful.

The customer you see in the professional environment may be different outside of the office. Don't be misled by this. The next day at the office or your next visit will be greeted by the original style you first encountered.

The chart on the following page will help you understand the prominent traits in each of these personality styles:

	The Enthusiast	The Dominator	The Moderator	The Analyst
Personality Style	Outgoing, engaging, people-oriented	Direct, dominant in conversation, sometimes imposing	Cooperative, affable. Relationships are important	Analytical, often black and white with no in-between
Speech	Lots of energy and inflection in the voice, enthusiastic	Deliberate with intention, not animated unless agitated	Pleasant, easy to speak with, affable, caring	Slow and reserved but speaks with confidence and conviction
Conversation	Upbeat, can wander off topic, sometimes doesn't listen well	To the point, short, brief, little time for things not relevant to the topic, looks for key points	Easy going, usually a pleasant flow. Easy to talk to. Will often times listen intently	Inquisitive, wants the information, will challenge your resources and claims
Body Language	Open, inviting	Straight, imposing	Inviting, comfortable	Reserved, inquisitive, arms folded
Organization	Scattered. Office cluttered and with pictures of favorite events	Organized. Office displays achievement awards and photos	Neat office, somewhat organized with family pictures and keepsakes	Everything in its place, plaques of validation displayed, sterile and not overly welcoming
Pace	Go with the flow, upbeat	Fast and deliberate, always on the move	Slow and steady, not in a hurry	Calculated and efficient
Decisions	Likely to go with the popular decision, based more on emotion than facts	Quick, decisive and does not second-guess	Can be indecisive. Wants to please everyone	Will gather all the facts and make a calculated decision
Time Management	Will often run over time because of off-topic conversation	Tries to fit too much in and often runs behind	Will make time, does not like to feel rushed	On time, little time for pleasantries
Dress	Often as casual as possible, sometime disheveled	Often sharply dressed and formal, making a statement usually of power or intent, well groomed	Somewhat neat as needed but not concerned about fashion	Neat, conservative, can be scholarly
Gestures	Gregarious, animated at times, using hands and arms frequently	Looks at clock, or watch, paces, taps hands	Not animated, can be measured depending on the topic or the tone from the other person	Closed, cold, arms folded, glasses low on nose on occasion

UNDERSTANDING THE FOUR PERSONALITY STYLES

The categories are not meant as labels for you or the people you are communicating with. They are not meant as stereotypes either. It's important to understand that *we are all a combination of these traits.* Some are simply more dominant than others and are adaptive depending on the environment.

For instance, as you look at the traits of someone who is more dominant in style, that person may exhibit those traits very strongly in a work environment, however when the pressure is off, at home the same person may still be engaging yet more laid back

The challenge is to identify the prominent traits in each situation where you are interacting. Understanding that person's prominent traits as well as your own will allow you to adapt to any situation. It will also allow you and the person you are communicating with to gain the most from the conversation and the entire interaction.

There are only four styles so they will be easy for you to remember and associate when you are communicating. The goal is to become able to recognize and adapt your style early enough in the discussion. If you accomplish this, you will find yourself receiving a great deal more information from each conversation and gaining the valuable insight needed to help your customer and to build stronger relationships. When people feel that you are genuinely interested in them, they will give you more time, they will likely want to see you again, and they will hold a higher opinion of you from that moment forward.

The personality styles we will consider are the *Enthusiast*, the *Dominator*, the *Moderator*, and the *Analyst*.

The Enthusiast

The personality style of the Enthusiast is generally outgoing, engaging, and people-oriented. The glass is half full. I label this style with the color blue because it correlates to the concept of "the sky is always blue." In the Enthusiast's world, the sky is the limit.

Enthusiasts are not loners. They enjoy social events with others who share common interests and are happy to talk. If you walk into an Enthusiast's office or home, you will see pictures of the activities they like.

I remember walking into an office and seeing a wonderful action photo of that person navigating whitewater rapids in a kayak. On another occasion I vividly remember walking into a materials manager's office in Bar Harbor, Maine, and seeing a panoramic view of the Boston Garden basketball court behind his desk.

From the outset, noticing these cues made it easy to determine what type of personality I was encountering, but you can't base your assessment on that alone. In conversation you may find that this person's true style is more direct and to the point than easy-going.

When you are speaking with an Enthusiast you will find they have lots of energy. It is apparent through their speech and the inflection in their voice. You will find the conversation to be upbeat. They will want to tell you about those whitewater rapids in the picture or the feeling of sitting at the Garden during a game... but be careful, they also tend to wander off topic and it can be a challenge to keep them focused on the reason you are there.

The Enthusiast's body language is often open and inviting. They will make you feel more relaxed and that will help you during a meeting with them, as long as you manage the time and veer conversation appropriately so you can accomplish your own objectives.

While on the opposite end of the spectrum, you would find someone with a more Analytical style with an office neat as a pin and nothing out of place, the Enthusiast's office may at times appear cluttered with file folders on the desk, and let's just say, not everything will be in its place.

The Enthusiast's pace is for the most part upbeat. They are optimistic about life and what it has to offer, and you can see that through their actions. Be aware that when it comes time for important group decisions, Enthusiasts may swing toward the popular vote and often make decisions based more on emotion than fact. They ultimately tend to go with the flow and will not make waves.

If you are in a conversation with an Enthusiast in his or her office, don't be surprised if your appointment runs long. You may start getting looks from the office staff. I have left an Enthusiast's office a time or two either drained from my futile attempts to stay on task, or thinking to myself, "What a nice person." But then later I realized I had accomplished absolutely nothing.

You must learn not to beat yourself up too much in those situations because sometimes things are just going to be out of your control. You may not always be able to constrain the flow of a conversation, but you will leave a conversation with more than you came with if you too have the cup-is-half-full attitude.

Two other important traits that distinguish an Enthusiast are dress and gestures. The Enthusiast is often more casual in appearance and sometimes disheveled. They may not always wear a tie or have their shoes polished, and they aren't so concerned about crisp starched shirts. Their non-verbal gestures will likely be gregarious, using their hands and arms to express themselves when they speak.

The Dominator

The Dominator is an individual who takes pride in being direct. You can quickly assess when you are in the presence of a Dominator because they naturally appear confident. You will see it in their entire posture. I use red to signify this style because it is a dominant color. My son-in-law just bought a red truck. When you are driving around in a red vehicle, you stand out in a crowd. The same is true for the Dominator.

The Dominator's style is one of confidence in conversation, and sometimes when challenged, this person can appear imposing. Their speech is deliberate and not necessarily animated, yet at times can be. You will also find that your conversations with a Dominator will be shorter and more to the point. Unlike the Enthusiast, they have little time for idle chit chat. Often they are so direct there will be little pause in between words or thoughts. In fact, it may be difficult to get a word in, so come prepared. When you speak with a Dominator, you must also be brief and to the point. They will appreciate that.

The Dominator's body language is not as relaxed as the Enthusiast. You will find them most often straight and confident in appearance. A Dominator's office will be organized. The pictures and plaques on the wall will be related to achievement and recognition rather than from outside hobbies or activities. That is not to say that the Dominator does not have hobbies or outside areas of interest, however they will not share them with just anyone in a work environment.

Sometimes your meeting with a Dominator may take the form of a fast-paced walk down a hall. The Dominator is a fast-paced individual. Throughout my sales career I can't tell you the number of times I have been in a conversation with a Dominator when I sensed they were literally about to be on the move. I simply said, "I know you must get going, so I'll walk with you." That always seemed to leverage the extra time I needed to finish the conversation. While in the orthopedic clinic in Bangor, Maine, I would often have discussions with surgeons, accompanying them as they walked from the hospital to their office in the building that was connected to the hospital. This was an efficient use of time for the Dominator and for me. On many occasions it was better than a planned appointment.

A Dominator is a great person to have in your camp when it comes time for major decisions. While a Dominator often makes quick and decisive decisions, they will also fight relentlessly for what they believe in. It is difficult to deter a Dominator who has strong conviction with regard to an issue they deem important, and is a good person to have in your court.

Drive is a key trait of the Dominator. Sometimes they try to fit too much into each day. They want to accomplish more than anyone else. Satisfaction comes from completion of tasks, turning vision into reality, and making their mark on the world.

In the Marine Corps, we had a phrase that was very Dominator-like in spirit. "We do more before 5:00 A.M. than the Army does all day." This competitive drive is prominent in the Dominator's approach to life. Like a good Marine, the Dominator wants to accomplish more than the competition.

The Dominator is sharply dressed, almost always formal in a business setting. He or she dresses with intent, making a clear statement of who they are. Don't be surprised if these fast-paced individuals frequently appear impatient, fidget with their hands, or look at their watch or the clock on the wall.

The Dominator personality trait is often found in the sales environment. Throughout my career, successful sales representatives tend to sway toward the Dominator or Enthusiast side, with a strong Analytical side squeaking into the picture mostly out of necessity.

It's important to understand that any one of these traits is not better than the others. It is not a rating scale. Being a Dominator does not determine whether you can be successful in sales or in communicating in general. All these style assessments do is give you clues about how someone else communicates... but more importantly as we will discuss shortly, it will show you how each personality style prefers to receive information.

The Moderator

The Moderator's color is green. The grass is green. I like you, you like me. The Moderator will not want to hurt your feelings even if they do not really like the product or what you are selling.

You will find the personality style of the Moderator to be cooperative, affable, and very pleasant. Relationships are important. It's sometimes difficult to read what a Moderator is really thinking. Remember, they don't want to hurt your feelings, and if you come on strong, you may inadvertently roll over them. They will continue to be kind and affable, but they may also tell their secretary or administrative assistant that they don't need to see you ever again after your appointment.

Conversation with a Moderator is usually very pleasant. They speak in moderate caring tones. Moderators will also listen intently. They are good at making you feel important and tend to focus on you. If your dominant traits are not that of a Moderator, you can certainly learn from this aspect of their behavior. Humans want to feel important no matter the predominant personality traits. Moderators are good at this.

You will find a Moderator's gestures to be inviting and friendly. A Moderator's office is generally neat and organized. Family pictures and cherished events with warm inviting colors tell the Moderator's life story. The Moderator is not in a hurry and does not like to be rushed. In fact, they may run overtime but they will do their best to stay on track if possible.

In conversation you will find the Moderator easy to speak with, but they can tend to ponder or at times appear indecisive. They want to weigh all the options when making a decision but can become torn because they don't want to hurt anyone's feelings. Unlike the Dominator who is very decisive and can be a huge advocate when fighting for a vital cause—such as getting your product accepted—a Moderator would rather let someone else make the decision so they can support the majority. Be careful hanging your hat on a Moderator in a crucial situation like the one just described; you may be disappointed in the end.

A Moderator's dress is on the conservative side, neat but not flashy, mostly unassuming. They prefer to stay under the radar. Their gestures mimic their apparel, conservative in nature. They tend not to be animated and will measure their tone accordingly in conversation but generally not above certain levels.

The Analyst

The Analyst is one of the most interesting and perhaps challenging for individuals of the other three traits to communicate with effectively. The Analyst is strong on data. They want all the facts and they look for black and white with very little in-between.

The Analyst's speech is crisp and direct. They speak with confidence and conviction and you can count on them having done their homework. But a word to the wise: don't show up unprepared or thinking you can wing it. If you do, you will find yourself winging it out the door.

If you capture the interest of an Analyst you will find them to be inquisitive and wanting more information. Don't be alarmed if they question or challenge your claims. Be prepared to back up what you present with solid data. The Analyst is particularly sensitive to the Four Pillars of *honesty, integrity, knowledge,* and *genuine interest.* They expect you to be knowledgeable, and their genuine interest will stem from their assessment of how and what you present to them based on their own perceived need.

You will find an Analyst to have very reserved body language. It takes time and validation of information for them to trust you so don't be surprised if their arms are folded and they appear to keep you at arm's length.

If you have ever walked into an Analyst's office you know it is absolutely neat with everything in its place. An Analyst can tell you exactly where each item is located. They pride themselves on their organizational skills.

The Analyst's pace is steady as she goes, calculated and efficient. Count on the Analyst to gather all the facts and analyze them before offering an opinion, coming to a conclusion, or making a decision. They expect you to be on time and they give little thought to pleasantries, although as you get to know them you will find that occurs briefly.

The Analyst is neat and can be scholarly in appearance. You can expect their gestures to be somewhat cold and reserved at first. I have actually attended meetings where Analysts prefer to speak to you while looking over their glasses, as if questioning what you say without even speaking a word.

Whatever your style is, make sure you adapt to the traits of an Analyst when encountering them, so that you leave no stone unturned and have total command of the facts. I am not asking you to become a chameleon, however. I am simply suggesting you should adjust your own preparation in order to communicate successfully.

In the next chapter we will dive deeper into creating effective communication between these four different styles.

SUMMARY

- If you understand your own personality style, you will find yourself effectively communicating with everyone you meet, and you will learn more about the people you interact with and yourself at the same time.

- The personality style of the Enthusiast is generally outgoing, engaging, and people-oriented.

- The Dominator takes pride in being direct. You will quickly assess when you are in the presence of a Dominator because they appear naturally confident.

- The Moderator is cooperative, affable, and very pleasant. Relationships are important to the Moderator, however, it's sometimes difficult to distinguish what a Moderator is really thinking.

- The Analyst is strong on data and analytics. They want all the facts and they look for black and white with very little in-between.

Chapter 8

Effective Communication in a Sales Call

While it takes seven seconds or less to make your first impression visually, that impression will either be confirmed or denied once you begin to speak. Effective communication starts with your ability to understand how to talk with other people based on their different personality traits.

As you probably noticed from the previous chapter, people of other styles than you may not appreciate your preferred method of communication. This is why the ability to adapt to other styles becomes important.

The good news is that you may already be doing this in everyday conversation without even thinking about it. You have friends of varying personality types and because you like each other, you most likely tolerate occasional personality and communication clashes. But in business, and on a sales call, you won't have that luxury. That's why it is so critical for you to understand communication models and become able to quickly adapt your approach to others.

First impressions are either confirmed or denied once you begin to speak.

In this section we will place different personality types together so you can get a feel for how to adjust in the future, and build a relationship by effectively communicating with that individual.

DOMINATOR MEETS THE ANALYST, MODERATOR, AND ENTHUSIAST

Dominator Meets the Dominator

If you are a Dominator your biggest challenge with all of the other traits is to just slow down. Even if you are working with another Dominator.

The challenge for any of us is to listen more than we speak, and when we do speak, to do so in a way that your customer understands and can find you credible and genuinely interested in what they have to say.

Dominators want to find salespeople they can trust, so they tend to build strong relationships with someone once they know they can count on them. They are no-nonsense and not full of second chances if you screw up. It will serve you well to know where their interests lie and study that area until you become well versed.

Speak and travel at their pace. In communicating with any style you should look for win-win, not I-win-and-you-lose. You may find yourself in a spirited conversation, and if you are also a Dominator you will welcome the opportunity.

Dominator Meets the Analyst

The Analyst wants detail, just the facts. If you are a Dominator attempting to communicate effectively with an Analyst, you will need to do your homework. The devil is in the details and if you don't have the details you won't be doing business with an Analyst.

The point is, even if you know the material and can answer the questions, the Analyst will not accept what you say at face value. The Analyst is a perfect example (as you will see later in the sales process chapter) of why it is so important to validate the features and benefits of your product or service with good credible and convincing data. The Analyst will demand it.

While other behavioral styles will take your word for many things and make a decision based on trust and strength of a relationship, the Analyst will make decisions based on their own research, and your credibility with them will be determined by the strength of the information you present.

The Dominator Meets the Enthusiast

While the Dominator and the Enthusiast are both high in energy, the Enthusiast is likely to stray off topic, making it difficult to stay on point. The challenge for any other style with the Enthusiast is to keep them focused. The challenge for the Dominator specifically, is to be able to move the Enthusiast into that lane where you can discuss things relevant to your objective during the sales call.

While the Dominator will want to get down to business, the more effective approach will be to weave in and out of a topic the Enthusiast wants to discuss while skillfully bringing it back around. If you do this abruptly, the Enthusiast could feel slighted. You will sense this as they become less and less engaged.

It's interesting, but by weaving something of interest to them alongside your objective for the meeting, the whole conversation will flow better, and you will feel that shift happen during the conversation. It is definitely an intangible aspect, but there, nonetheless.

The Dominator Meets the Moderator

The real danger for a Dominator when meeting a Moderator is in overpowering them. If you are a Dominator and feel you are communicating effectively with a Moderator, take another look. You could probably slow your pace even more.

While the Moderator will appreciate decisiveness, they will also be driven away and disengage quickly if you come in like a Ferrari when a Subaru Outback may be the more preferred pace.

The Moderator is more likely to want to get to know you... and they will want to do that at their own pace. Their decision-making process is weighed heavily on the feeling they have about you. If they like you, they may actually be looking for reasons to do business with you, however, if they feel uncomfortable, they will not want to see you again.

You may not even recognize such a shift during the meeting, but once you have left you may find it difficult or even impossible to arrange another appointment.

Slow your pace, listen, and pause before responding, then even paraphrase what they have said so they know you are listening.

The Dominator Meets the...

Analyst		Moderator
Have command of the facts		Don't overpower them
Don't rush through the information		Slow your speech accordingly
Be aware of their time constraints		Listen and do not cut them off
Don't force a closing statement		Paraphrase what they said ("If I understand what you are saying...")
Summarize and clearly define next steps		Take the time to build rapport
Enthusiast		Dominator
Show an interest in them		Move as fast as they do
Let them talk about themselves		Stay on track
Keep them focused without being too direct		Don't try too hard to build a relationship
Don't get frustrated with wandering topics		Don't try to overpower them. Just keep pace
Make enough time for them		Know that the conversation may be spirited

THE ANALYST MEETS THE DOMINATOR, ENTHUSIAST, AND MODERATOR

The Analyst Meets the Analyst

Analysts want all the facts, are generally well versed in their own area of expertise, and pride themselves on having command of the data. If you are an Analyst speaking with another Analyst, your challenge is to not get into a battle of facts, because you can't win.

They will appreciate your knowledge and your preparedness because that is what they expect, however your mission is not to challenge them but to provide well thought out fact-based solutions to the needs you uncover during the sales process.

You may more often than not be challenged on your claims, as you will see when you validate your own product claims with your own data.

As an Analyst, you will be less likely to rush, though you will need to summarize clearly and be specific with next steps.

The Analyst Meets the Moderator

The Moderator poses a challenge to the Analyst because the Moderator may not counter any of the data presented. They may even appear to agree, however internally that may not be the case for them.

As an Analyst, your pace may be more in line with theirs than a Dominator or Enthusiast, but you must also be able to show empathy. Remember, a Moderator wants to find a reason to like and do business with you. Asking them how they feel about the data you used to validate your product will go a long way to getting feedback as opposed to assuming they are buying into what you are saying.

In the end, don't make things so black and white. Take the time to build the relationship and go the distance to make sure the

Moderator feels like you understand them and their needs clearly.

To a Moderator, your knowledge and command of the facts will go much further if it is attached to a strong relationship.

The Analyst Meets the Dominator

The Dominator is always on the move, fast paced, and often direct. The challenge then for the Analyst is to be able to keep up. While as an Analyst you just want to spew out all that knowledge and data, you will never have the opportunity with a Dominator because they just want the cliff notes version.

An Analyst can be very valuable to a Dominator if the Analyst builds rapport and trust quickly. In fact, as the relationship grows, a Dominator will appreciate having a go-to Analyst in their camp. They know the value of a good Analyst and, with trust in that relationship, will count on that person to provide them with the facts needed to make product-related decisions.

The Analyst should never take this for granted though. That is not to say the Dominator will never do fact checks, relying solely on a relationship, however it is an honor to be held in that regard by a high performance Dominator.

The Analyst Meets the Enthusiast

An Analyst may struggle the most with an Enthusiast. The Enthusiast, while interested in the facts, may not want to engage in a technical discussion.

The Enthusiast, like the Dominator, may prefer the cliff notes version, but not because they are moving at such a fast pace but rather because they have other things to talk about not related necessarily to the topic at hand.

If you are an Analyst, this can be frustrating because after all, you know so much about the product and the data, and you want to get it all out. But in the case of the Enthusiast, the Analyst must allow the conversation to stray off the reservation for a few minutes at a time when it comes to details, then strategically select the appropriate time to reinforce the value of their knowledge and data, while communicating the information to fill the customer's need or find a solution to an issue for the Enthusiast.

The Analyst should be willing to engage in conversation in order to show interest to the Enthusiast, trusting that the time for facts, data, and product validation will come.

The Analyst Meets the...

Analyst		Moderator
Have command of the facts		Slow down to their pace
Don't rush through the information		Slow your speech accordingly
Be aware of their time		Listen and do not cut them off
Don't force a closing statement		Paraphrase what they said ("If I understand what you are saying...")
Summarize and clearly define next steps		Take the time to build the relationship
Enthusiast		Dominator
Adjust to their pace		Move as fast as they do
Show an interest in them		Don't overuse data
Let them talk		Stick to the key points that satisfy their need
Keep them focused without being too direct		Don't continue to sell when they are ready to buy
Don't get frustrated with wandering topics		Know that the conversation may be spirited

THE MODERATOR MEETS THE DOMINATOR, ENTHUSIAST, AND ANALYST

The Moderator Meets the Dominator

The challenge for a Moderator in many circumstances is to pick up the pace. The Moderator must use a lot more energy to adapt to different styles. When communicating with a Dominator, the Moderator has to flip the intensity switch in order to keep up. If they don't, the conversation won't last long at all.

Some Dominators are so fast paced you actually have to walk beside them as they move to their next appointment or meeting.

As a Moderator it's important to choose the best time and place for a conversation, then be keenly aware of the time and make sure you have reviewed the meeting in your mind before it happens.

Know that the conversation may be up-tempo and spirited. Stay on your game, however, and don't act like you are not up to the task. The Dominator won't respect that. Make sure you have a grasp of your key points and be as brief and to the point as possible.

The Moderator Meets the Analyst

The Moderator can adapt effectively to the Analyst because the pace is slower, however the Analyst is going to be crisp, direct, and to the point. The challenge as a Moderator is to present the facts clearly, and be up for the challenge when it comes to validation of product.

While the Moderator has command of the facts, they also must be able to stand behind those facts and not find themselves agreeing with an Analyst just to avoid confrontation.

If you are a Moderator, chances are you are already able to build rapport effectively, but at the same time you must be willing to step outside your comfort zone when it is time to present information, and then do so with conviction. The Analyst will sense immediately whether you really have a command of the facts. Stay on point and summarize effectively.

The Moderator Meets the Moderator

The Moderator meeting the Moderator can be more complicated than it first appears. The good thing is that you both will try hard to like each other. The bad news is that you will avoid each other if you find you don't.

The challenge is to keep the meeting moving while spending plenty of time to enhance rapport. You can't switch into Dominator mode and expect to be successful.

Be patient, be prepared, and make sure if possible to have notes that encompass the scope of the conversation. This will allow you to leave the meeting satisfied that you have accomplished your objectives while making sure there was enough time spent to address the needs of the customer. This is especially important to a Moderator.

The Moderator Meets the Enthusiast

The Moderator will be challenged with bringing the Enthusiast back on topic because they won't want to interrupt. After all, that wouldn't be polite.

Seriously, the Moderator has the greatest chance of leaving a meeting with an Enthusiast without having moved to the next step. It may have seemed like a great meeting but in the end nothing got accomplished.

If you are a Moderator, it's important to summarize the points at the beginning of the meeting and to again close the meeting with a summary of next steps, otherwise you may find yourself in your car saying, "What a great meeting," but have accomplished nothing because rather than agreeing on next steps, you only agreed the Patriots were better than the Chiefs (at least at the time of this writing), or whatever your favorite teams happen to be.

The Moderator Meets the...

Analyst		Moderator
Have command of the facts		Match their pace
Don't rush through the information		Take the time to build rapport
Be aware of their time		Show *genuine interest* in them and their needs
Be confident in delivery of information		Avoid restating information unless necessary
Summarize and clearly define next steps		Clarify next steps before leaving
Enthusiast		Dominator
Adjust to their pace		Move as fast as they do
Show an interest in them		Don't wander off topic
Let them talk about themselves		Stick to the key points that satisfy their need
Don't forget what you came to accomplish		Be clear, concise, and brief
Do not interrupt. Summarize at the beginning and the end		Know that the conversation may be spirited

THE ENTHUSIAST MEETS THE DOMINATOR, ANALYST, AND MODERATOR

The Enthusiast Meets the Dominator

If there ever was a stereotype for salespeople, such as the person with the gift of gab or the person who followed the customer down the hall talking even after the door was shut in front of them, that might be the Enthusiast.

The greatest challenge for the Enthusiast with any of the other styles—but especially the Dominator—is to stay on message. Another challenge is to be prepared, providing the cliff note version if needed, and to be clear and to the point. Engage in outside topics only if led by the Dominator.

It's not that there will never be a time to engage in idle chat with a Dominator, but those instances will be few and far between, especially in a professional setting. At dinner or a function it will be different. Those are instances where an Enthusiast may shine in conversation with a Dominator, however during a sales call, it is important to stay on message.

The most important thing to remember about a Dominator is that they are driven, while as an Enthusiast it is easy to wander off topic. If you are an Enthusiast speaking with a Dominator, adapt by being direct, brief, and less of a storyteller.

The Enthusiast Meets the Analyst

The initial meeting between an Enthusiast and an Analyst could end up being oil and water if not approached thoughtfully. If you are an Enthusiast, store the mountain bike in the garage and table the weekend football standings for good solid data needed to validate your product along with the benefits that will solve issues or needs of your Analyst customer.

This is not to suggest the Analyst never mountain bikes or likes football, they just by nature want to stick to the facts. There will always be time for the other conversations... just not in a sales call. That is unless they engage you. If they do, still be reserved and do not use it as a license to stray far from the reasons you are there. You may find yourself with no time left and scrambling to talk about your product and the reason you were there in the first place.

The Enthusiast Meets the Moderator

The Moderator is very affable, as can be most Enthusiasts. If you are an Enthusiast you are generally more fast paced than a Moderator and you tend to tell stories. The Moderator will also generally listen.

Many Enthusiasts who wander off topic will fail to realize that they are not being well received. This is the challenge of the Enthusiast when conversing with other styles. It is even more so with the Moderator because the Moderator will go with the flow and may even engage in conversation, however it may also be your last meeting with them unless you are cautious.

Make the meeting more about them and engage in conversations they are interested in, as opposed to talking about yourself. Always stay close to the reason you are there in the first place and do your best to speak at their pace.

The Enthusiast Meets the Enthusiast

This is an administrative assistant's nightmare. Two individuals left alone in a room who love to talk. If you are also an Enthusiast the challenge for you is to let them talk more about themselves rather than turning their story into a similar one of your own.

It is already difficult for an Enthusiast to stay on schedule, so you won't be doing either of you any favors by not paying attention to the value of their time. Save the long version of stories for a social meeting or a business dinner where a personal story will add value to building rapport.

Another major challenge for the Enthusiast salesperson is getting around to asking for the business at the appropriate time. If you can't stay on point and forget this important step, don't be surprised if your competitor who happens to be a Dominator asks this Enthusiast for the sale and gets it.

The Enthusiast Meets the...

Analyst		Moderator
Have command of the facts		Slow down to their pace
Don't rush through the information		Slow your speech accordingly
Be aware of their time		Listen and do not cut them off
Don't wander off topic		Avoid talking about yourself and instead ask about them
Summarize and clearly define next steps		Take the time to build the relationship
Enthusiast		Dominator
Adjust to their pace		Move as fast as they do
Show an interest in them		Don't wander off topic
Do not interrupt		Stick to the key points that satisfy their need
Let them talk about themselves		Be clear, concise, and brief
Don't forget what you came to accomplish		Know that the conversation may be spirited

Each personality style will have their own way of determining whether you have abided by the Four Pillars.

The first seven seconds say a lot about you, but the things you do and say from that point on will allow any personality style to assess and draw conclusions about whether you are being *honest*, have the capacity to do the right thing (your *integrity*), whether you are *knowledgeable* about the subject and the industry, and whether you are *genuinely interested* in them and have their best interests at heart.

SUMMARY

- We are all different and we all have personality styles that vary.

- It is critical for you to quickly understand the personality type of the person you are communicating with.

CHAPTER 9
FINDING COMMON GROUND

When you are in a sales environment you are going to meet all types of people. Some you are going to like, and others not. Some you will do business with for a long time, and others never. One thing is certain though, if you become a student of life and people in general, you will become a lifelong learner. A lifelong learner isn't just someone who attends seminars and reads a lot of books. No, a lifelong learner recognizes that every individual has something to offer, and by finding out more about them and their story, it makes your own stories that much more complete.

I have had countless dinners with customers and been on numerous sales calls—alone or with salesmen I have helped along the way. The one thing I am so grateful for is that I have taken something from every meeting. If you open yourself up to a *genuine interest* in each customer, you will find yourself telling a story somewhere down the line relevant to that prior conversation. If you have done a good job building your relationship, then your story becomes *believable, credible*, and shows that you are *knowledgeable* in your field. Showing *genuine interest* and establishing common ground makes people and moments memorable. It can turn a meeting into a lasting relationship.

A sales representative for our company asked me to attend a dinner meeting many years ago. The surgeon customer learned that I had spent much of my life in Maine. He shared that he liked hunting and fishing, so I told him about the log cabin I built and shared that I liked to fly fish for trout. He liked to fly fish too, and within minutes we had found common ground and began to build trust as the conversation flowed.

I genuinely liked this person and I know the dinner went on much longer than we expected. Eventually we did get around to talking about what products he used in his practice and I was able to ask questions in a very non-threatening and non-canned way about his long-term goals and ambitions for his practice.

Finding out how he wanted to make purchases was valuable. He was in a very competitive area and he really wanted to grow and establish a name for himself. We have since run into each other at meetings many times throughout the years and we always seem to talk about the latest trip or a fly that just killed them on a spring morning early in the season.

The salesman who had originally invited me along to that dinner asked me, "How did you do that?" ...to which I replied, "What?" He said, "That conversation just went so well."

I believe you can find common ground with anyone if you just listen, show genuine interest, and don't try too hard.

Open yourself up to a genuine interest in each customer.

The Four Pillars weave their way into all conversations. If you're being *honest* with yourself, you will find yourself speaking more confidently, and while *integrity* is largely based on what you do, people begin to get a sense of that, even after first meeting you. The pillars of *knowledge* and *genuine interest* allow you to build on any conversation and lead you to the common ground needed to establish the foundation of a good and lasting relationship.

When I was a young salesman traveling in the farthest reach of Maine, I had three customers north of Bangor. One was in Millinocket, and another in Caribou was a French-Canadian surgeon to whom I owe a lot because he toughened me up. I learned enough to be confident in talking about my products to new customers through him. Jean-Pierre (J.P.) Michaud held my feet to the fire and I am better for it. We spent a lot of good times together and I'll be forever in debt for all I learned in those early years.

The third was a new surgeon, Pat Fallon, and in 1995 I couldn't get into the office to see him. I also couldn't even get near the operating room because the O.R. supervisor had a good relationship with the then-current sales rep and wasn't about to let me in the door. Letting me in the door would have introduced the possibility of change, and potential change is what people fear and hate most!

One late February afternoon when I had a four-hour drive ahead of me to get home, I was driving through the next closest town of Presque Isle. I came to the stoplight at Academy Street on Route 1. It was 5:00 P.M. and just about dark. I sat there contemplating whether to go straight or turn left.

At that very moment the light changed, I made a decision to turn left and go to Pat's office. As I drove up, the lights were all off except for one in the back. A small Ford was parked in the lot. Shaking, I went up to the office door which was inside an enclosed porch. The building used to be an old home. After several knocks and almost walking away, Dr. Fallon came out of the darkness, still dictating as he opened the door.

I had no way out now, so I had to say something as he stared at me. Those first seven seconds felt like an eternity.

I eventually said, "I'm really sorry to bother you. My name is Gerry Savage and I'm your local Zimmer Rep." He looked at me and said, "Come on back, I'm almost done. Zimmer, eh?" he said. "I'm Zimmerized." Pat was Canadian from Fredericton, New Brunswick.

When he finished his dictation, we had the best conversation that went from his wife who was just about to have a baby, to hockey, and to orthopedics. We found common ground in minutes. I never had trouble seeing him again and I always appreciated his time. I know I can pick up the phone even today and we can have a great conversation. That one evening changed my career. I took a chance, even though I was scared, but to this day we remain close friends. As a side note, the hospital where Dr. Fallon performed all of his cases went from about $8,000 per year with my company to over $750,000 the following year.

When you wake up tomorrow, you are one day closer to realizing your sales goals.

People sense whether you are sincere or not but many will also give you the benefit of the doubt and let your actions speak for themselves. The old adage "Fool me once, shame on you, but fool me twice, shame on me" is something you may have experienced already. If you are genuinely interested in what people have to say, they will sense that and become more at ease. It allows you to establish the common ground needed to build a relationship. Without that, it's just a conversation that will be long forgotten in a short time.

Learn the lessons of yesterday well. They hold the key to your future and your destiny. Remember when you wake up tomorrow you are one day closer to realizing your sales goals.

Find common ground with the people you meet and show a *genuine interest* in them. You will be surprised and blessed by the relationships that can and will come from such an attitude. You will touch people's lives and it will make you stronger in the pursuit of your own goals and dreams. So knock on that door.

SUMMARY

- The Four Pillars weave their way into every conversation.
- If you have *genuine interest* in people, you will find common ground.
- Common ground allows you to build a relationship.
- Learn the lessons of yesterday well. They hold the key to your future and your destiny.

PART THREE

The Sales Process

CHAPTER 10

THE SALES PLANNING PROCESS

So now that we've talked about your view of selling, your belief in yourself, your belief in your product, your belief in your abilities, understanding all the different personality types you might encounter, and how important it is to establish common ground, you're probably wondering when I am going to get to the point! What about a sales process... where do we begin, and how do we use it?

As you've already learned, great selling has a lot in common with great storytelling. The tools you've gathered in previous chapters can now be put into action.

"If you don't have a plan, you plan to fail," may not always be true in the short-term—because many seem to get by in spite of themselves—but after the initial spurt of energy, those who lack a plan will let things go and only step back up when it all starts to fall apart.

I remember a distributor who had been with the company for just about a year, but he'd been working in orthopedics for over 20 years. I met with him mainly because his quarterly business review was not what he and I expected it to be, and his presentation to the company had not gone well. He had over-projected early on and had not delivered.

Sound familiar? He also had several young sales reps, and I think he underestimated the amount of coaching they would require. I also believe he was more of a father figure to those young sales reps than a true leader. This is not an indictment because I think many heads of organizations are in the same position, becoming more patriarchal—a father figure, as opposed to a leader.

As we got into our discussion, I realized that while he had a framework of a plan for the sales reps, he had no plan for accountability. The reps had no sense of what was required from them. Was it sales calls and the activities necessary to grow business, or was something else preventing them from growing their current business and bringing new customers on board?

This is what needs to take place when you have a plan, but they are only pieces; by themselves, they are not the plan.

There are many ways to interpret what a plan is, but when it comes down to it, a plan is your roadmap to success.

If you enter a square patch of woods from the center of one side and you intend to exit on the road directly opposite where you entered, how could you do that without a map of the terrain and a compass? Maybe if you were lucky on a sunny day and knew how to use the sun to track your progress you could make it, but what if it was cloudy? It becomes more difficult without a doubt.

My dad, who was great in the woods, used to take me hunting every year when I was a kid in the big North Maine Woods. We would stay in an old hunting camp about three miles off the main road. Behind our camp was a large cedar swamp, which was more difficult to navigate, especially on cloudy days. As fate would have it, on one of these cloudy and snowy mornings, we entered the woods behind the camp. After several hours of walking, my dad stopped and looked up at a piece of metal in a tree which we had passed sometime during the day.

I instantly said, "What's the matter?" after seeing the look on his face. He said, "Well, we've just walked in a big circle." He'd thought we were walking in a straight line.

I was pretty scared, but my dad took out his compass and it instantly became near and dear to his heart and mine. He picked a direction and followed it, then checked the compass constantly. Hours later, much after dark, we came out on a connecting road that led to the camp about two miles away.

The point is, having a plan should not be an option. The plan will be your roadmap. But you still have to execute it by taking action steps toward your objective. There is no doubt you must use your compass along the way to make course corrections. Course adjustments are a fact of life.

The shortest distance between two points is a straight line, but it's okay to be on either side of the line as long as you use the compass to get back on course. In this case, your map becomes your business plan. While it may not be etched in stone, your compass—the ability to continually evaluate what's working while your plan is in motion—can be used to check progress and see if you are still on course. If you are not, there's no need to complain or lament. Simply make a course correction.

This plan, just like a map, begins as a static model. It will show you only where you need to go, but you will have to make corrections in order to hit your objective. Without the map, you and your compass will be at the mercy of all factors outside of your control, much like a ship without a rudder—at the mercy of the wind, the sea, and changing tides.

It's okay to veer off the path as long as you use a compass to get back on course.

I came to an agreement with that distributor whose early projections had not been borne out. We worked together and implemented a plan that he could use with his sales reps. Your company may already have a business plan that you update every year. If they do, welcome it, but you should also look at your own personalized plan or perhaps a version of the company's plan, along with your personal objectives.

Consider these points in your sales planning process:

1. What is realistic?
2. Don't over-project.
3. Revisit your plan regularly.
4. Consider realistic timeframes.
5. Use your compass to make course corrections as needed.
6. Replace bad targets with more realistic ones as your plan develops throughout the year.
7. Use all the necessary and available resources to execute your plan.
8. Hold yourself accountable to your plan.

SUMMARY

- When you don't have a plan, it's like you're planning to fail.

- Your plan is your roadmap to success. You will need both short-term and long-term plans.

- Plan your execution, then hold yourself accountable to it.

- If you are off course, make adjustments.

CHAPTER 11

THE SALES PROCESS

There are hundreds of companies out there that have defined the sales process in their own way. Some like Dale Carnegie and Sandler Training, and even Integrity Selling, are well respected and have trained thousands upon thousands of sales associates.

But what are we trying to do here? It's easy for a process to become canned in its delivery. It's kind of like taking a test, right? You study and study and you cram and cram, and then on exam day, you try to get the answers right.

In school, it's generally a multiple choice, or sometimes an essay, and you hope you can remember enough good content. But this isn't a canned presentation. This isn't an essay you will have to recite. The sales process should come from inside you.

Just like I can't sell you anything unless you have a need for it, which we will talk about later, you can't internalize the sales process *unless you understand it.*

You can't internalize the sales process unless you understand it.

If you understand something and you understand it well, what you say may come out different every time, however, the message will still remain the same.

This is not like that children's game where someone whispers something in the first person's ear and the message gets passed down the line... until by the time you get to the end, the message has changed completely. But your message won't change, because once you've internalized the sales process, whether you're on the front end or the back end of that line—and no matter how you actually verbalize it—the message will be the same, and hopefully so will your outcome.

The process is not as complicated as you might think, and it doesn't need to be canned or packaged in a way that if you miss something along the way, it's just going to fall apart.

The process we are about to discuss includes the Introduction, the Discussion, and within that Discussion a Feature-Benefit conversation. Following the Feature-Benefit portion, you must Validate your claims with supporting data about the product that fulfills the customer's need. Objections are likely to surface at any time, and you will need to be prepared to handle them if you expect to move the process forward. Following that, you get to move to the all-important Close, which you will find is really not the close of anything, but rather the beginning of a long and lasting relationship that is mutually beneficial to all parties.

The Sales Process

HONESTY

INTEGRITY

1. Introduction

(transition zone)

2. Discussion
including Feature-Benefit

(transition zone)

3. Validation

(transition zone)

4. Close

KNOWLEDGE

GENUINE INTEREST

The process is also where the Four Pillars will shine through for you: *honesty*—with yourself and others, by providing fact-based information, *integrity*—following through by doing what you say you will do, *knowledge*—by being a student of your industry so you can understand how your product or service can benefit the customer, and finally, *genuine interest*—the pillar that shows you care.

SALES PROCESS: THE INTRODUCTION

The introduction is the space that allows you to find common ground and to determine the personality profile of the person you are speaking with. Whether you have previously met the potential customer or not, it is still the initial step and it sets the stage for what follows.

During the Introduction, there is a lot going on other than just an exchange of words and pleasantries. If you have met the customer before, hopefully you will have had a chance to review the personality assessment to determine that person's profile ahead of time. In this case you will already be prepared to deliver your information in a way your customer can best receive it. If you haven't met them previously then you should have your detective hat on.

When you first meet someone, it's usually a handshake, or if somebody's not into handshakes these days because of a fear of germs, then maybe it's an elbow. Who knows? But the main thing is that when you approach someone and extend your hand, be positive and most of all be yourself.

When you enter an office, look for clues. These clues will give you insight into the customer's personality profile. You are not doing this to be nosy, or to put one over on anyone. You are simply looking for clues that will enable you to understand your customer better so that as you transition to a Discussion, you and your customer can have meaningful dialogue. This way you both get the most out of the conversation.

Don't comment on things simply to make up dead space in a conversation though, and don't ask about things you really have no interest in. When you have meaningful dialogue with genuine interest in your customer, you set the stage for identifying a need that he or she has. This will also make it easier to uncover common interests. Remember the fourth pillar—*genuine interest*. If you are not genuine, it will come across and people will sense this quickly.

Once you understand what their profile is and are able to adapt, then you can move on or transition into asking the appropriate questions to **identify a need** they know they have, or that they may not know they have. But first, let's see how we get there.

Let's suppose for a minute that you are meeting a customer for the very first time. That person is new to the area and just beginning to test the waters. When you walk into his office you see he has pictures of his favorite college football team on the wall along with pictures of whitewater rafting and pictures with family and friends on a hiking trip out west. Also displayed directly behind the desk are certificates of his many accomplishments. The desk is somewhat neat, but not neat as a pin.

When you meet him in the lobby, he invites you inside and asks if you want coffee or anything to drink. Then he walks quickly, giving the impression that he is busy. While pleasant enough, this person is quick to tell you what he uses and why all of his patients are doing great.

What personality traits could you identify immediately? And what clues helped you identify that?

- Outgoing, extroverted, engaging in conversation
- Asked you back to his office and offered you a beverage
- Pictures indicated he was proud of his accomplishments
- Spoke directly and with little pause

This person has a couple of traits that stand out. First, he is driven. He walks and talks at a quick pace. He is highly motivated and extremely proud of his accomplishments and will waste little time in telling you about them once he is asked. Because he has a more Dominator leaning personality rather than a moderate-paced fully outgoing and expressive type of individual, you will want to consider the following in the flow of the conversation:

- Be very aware of the time you have, and make sure you use it wisely without going over your allotment.

- While he has some outgoing, affable traits, you will find this individual direct and to the point, and maybe even somewhat set in his ways.

- Be as brief as possible. You will not have time to sit and review clinical article after article to substantiate your product claims.

- You can make your product claims as you move in to Features and Benefits following the Discussion period, but you will not be able to go into every detail.

- You should have the material but be so well versed that you can state things such as the type of study or studies used to substantiate the use of your product. This person may or may not review it later.

You should be able to assess all of this and more in the first few minutes of your meeting. Once you do, it's time for you to make the adjustments in your personality style in order to communicate effectively.

If you are the same style as the person you are meeting, then you will need to dial it back just enough to let him speak without jumping in too soon. As you transition from the Introduction into the Discussion phase, which we will talk about next, your understanding of your customer's personality profile will determine how you use and deliver your product information.

The important thing to take away is your ability to adapt your style to communicate with that of your customer. By knowing your customer and understanding how they receive information, you will figure out what adjustments to make to be most effective. Sometimes it's not easy, and depending on the differences in your styles, you may come out of the meeting mentally exhausted because of the amount of energy you had to bring out... or restrain.

Let's look at one more scenario and let's assume for a minute that you are a Dominator and your new potential customer is on the Analytical side of the curve.

When you walk into this customer's practice, you are greeted and brought back to the doctor's office by one of the assistants. The client is not there yet so you are left to look around a quiet room. You notice there is not one thing out of place and not one folder on the desk even though you are sure this surgeon is seeing about 70 patients today and will still be dictating after everyone in the office has gone home. There are awards and certificates on the wall and one family picture on the credenza which houses a collection of hardcover medical reference books, all neat and in place. Your homework told you that this person is fellowship-trained and has submitted or participated in several recent journal publications.

When she enters, she takes a seat behind her desk, folds her hands, and looks intently across at you.

Some things you should be picking up right away are:

- This person is analytical, less outgoing, and not quick to engage in conversation.

- This person is willing to let you into her office which is her domain, neat as a pin, almost sterile.

- Her posture alone (hands folded, leaning forward) asks somewhat defensively, "Why are you here? Should I trust you?"

- Based on what you see around the office, she is not inviting you to ask questions about her personal life. She wants to stick to the facts.

- You should be keenly aware of the time you are taking up in her day.

- She will take the time to listen to you if she feels you are competent, and you are presenting something that she finds interesting and relevant.

- You will need to be well prepared to substantiate your claims.

- And you will need to slow down, given your own style. Speak clearly. Provide only the information that solves a problem or fills a need. Be careful in the use of unsubstantiated claims as evidence because they will not be accepted and may even show up potentially as an objection.

What if instead, you and your customer are both Moderators, very amiable and affable? You like everyone and so does she. She moves slowly, takes more time with people and is always glad to see old friends and meet new reps. She wants to find out just as much about you as you do about her. If you're not careful, her staff will be giving you dirty looks because she wants to keep talking, even when lunch has been over for ten minutes. This is where you should be very careful. One thing I have learned—especially as the level of stress and anxiety begin to pile on—is that we tend to go where we are most liked and most well received. I call these *milk runs* because they are routine, non-threatening, and make us feel good. But beware of the milk run. These types of customers really won't do anything to help you grow new business.

When you go into a sales call, adapt your style to communicate effectively, and make your points in enough detail to substantiate why this person needs your product (or to make a change from something he or she is currently using). Be aware that a yes may not be a yes. It may be a way of not hurting your feelings, or the feelings of the current rep if that isn't you.

A few years ago, I went along on a sales call with one of my sales reps to meet a surgeon in Alexandria, Virginia. This surgeon had been to our corporate office for a visit and performed a total knee procedure on a cadaver specimen. He loved everything he saw and said, "Now all I have to do is find the right patient."

That was the first flag, but I was willing to give him the benefit of the doubt. Needless to say, months had gone by, and on this one day my sales rep and I went to his office for lunch. Since I wasn't intimately involved with the customer like the rep was on a regular basis, I was able to ask a few more direct questions. I asked the surgeon if he liked the technology and if he saw a benefit to his patients. I also asked him if he was comfortable with the instruments or if he needed to see something else.

Your customer's personality type should dictate not only the types of questions you ask, but how you frame them.

He said, "No, I think I'm good." So at this point I asked again, "Is there anything else holding you back from booking a case?" This wonderful easy going man all of a sudden showed a degree of pain on his face and in the loudest tone I had ever heard him speak said, "You guys just don't understand how hard it is for someone to switch." *Bingo.* The place he was coming from was a spot-on Moderator. "I like you, you like me. I like my other rep too, and can't we just be friends? Maybe someday I'll try one."

Of course, that would mean his other rep would have to switch companies, leave town, or something along those lines. You get the picture.

Things for you to look for when coming into this person's office or meeting for the first time:

- Will the person take a lot of time with you?
- Is the person interested in hearing what other customers are doing?
- Does this person speak slowly and thoughtfully?
- Is the person very interested in you?
- Does the person like to show you some of his cases?
- Is the office organized, or cluttered?
- Is this person often very non-committal?

The key to building any relationship, and the key to ultimately closing any sale, starts with how good a job you've done in your Introduction to understand your client or prospect so you can build a long-term relationship. These relationships are built on mutual understanding and respect. Remember that... *mutual understanding and respect.* You can't build this kind of bond unless you communicate effectively, and communication must run in both directions.

THE INTRODUCTION CAN OPEN OR CLOSE THE DOOR

Most every sales process or training talks about attention-getting questions in the Introduction, and open-ended questions in the Discussion—sometimes called an interview. I never really fell in love with the word *interview* because it made me think of an interrogation, and no one except a prisoner is going to sit there and let you interrogate them! The term *Discussion* feels better as it implies that input and feedback is coming from both parties.

Of course, you could ask a closed-ended yes or no question when you get to the... you guessed it... the infamous Close.

The personality type of the customer is going to dictate not only the type of questions you ask but how you frame them.

For instance, you walk into an office for the first time and your customer sits down. Before you can get your next breath, the prospect asks, "What brings you in today?" or says, "I've only got a few minutes, what can I do for you?"

You may have little time to build rapport so you may find that the rapport building comes instead through skillfully bringing information into the Discussion. In fact with this type of individual, you may be doing a limited Introduction and jumping right into the Discussion. This is another reason why first impressions are important. I believe rapport is built both verbally and non-verbally. You may have been sized up even before you began to speak, and sometimes, let's face it, we are all visual. If the customer doesn't like what they see, you may not have a chance.

In each of these situations, your ability to quickly assess what personality type you are speaking will determine whether the meeting will last just long enough for you to get escorted out the door or if you can transition to a Discussion.

The dialogue that follows may sound a bit like that canned presentation we vowed to avoid, but I include it here to bring to light the fact that if you never ask the questions, the conversation will likely go nowhere—or in a direction dictated by the customer rather than you. This dialogue is included only to give you a framework for later forming your own questions, in your own words, the way you would normally ask them.

Generally, if I was able to maintain my composure, I would say, "I appreciate your time so I will be brief." The person will automatically think, "Okay, I guess I can listen for just a minute." He may even say, "Great, because I only have about ten minutes."

If you have done your research—which I'm sure you have because you wouldn't be there wasting the prospect's time, right?—you might say, "What do you think is most important to surgeons today: better outcomes, lower length of stay, or just the ability to do more cases? Feel free to add what you would like if any of those don't make sense."

This is not a yes or no question and you are going to get one of any number of answers. Here are just a few:

- "I think many surgeons want to do more cases."

- "I think our outcomes are good today. We've come a long way."

- "Outpatient surgery is definitely going to increase rapidly over the next few years, so I would like to do more outpatient cases."

There are many ways to build on these comments, and it could go in several directions, but the important thing is that you now have a dialogue going... a conversation.

Follow-up questions might be:

- "What would help you get to more outpatient cases?"

- "I'm happy your outcomes are good. What would even better outcomes look like?"

- "Why do you feel same-day surgery is on the rise?"

Introductions to a new customer can be the most intense or stressful part of the process. I have found that questions which are asked about an issue on a broader scale—not necessarily specific to the individual with whom I'm speaking—reveals answers to the individual's own issues more honestly.

In the above example, I could have asked, "What's more important *to you* as a surgeon: better outcomes, lower length of stay, or just the ability to do more cases?" The first example, however, allows the person to respond more freely without feeling like they are being interrogated. It allows the dialogue to transition with more open communication.

You will find that as you get beyond the Introduction though, the tensions will ease, especially if you use the tools at your disposal to understand your customer and how they communicate.

THINGS TO WATCH FOR IN DIFFERENT PERSONALITY STYLES

- A **Dominator** will want you to get to the point but won't want to dig down into clinical research. Establish rapport by speaking up to their level but not over. Walk at their pace, which you will find yourself doing because the conversation may take place while walking from one meeting to the next. Don't be afraid to say, "I'll walk with you," because as long as you're not holding them up, you may by surprised by what you can accomplish. This may be a challenge if you are more affable and low-key. It may also be difficult if you are analytical, because your tendency would be to share more information than the Dominator wants or can handle in that moment.

- An **Analyst** will listen to everything you say. It's important to make sure you have your facts correct and avoid too many "I don't know but I'll find out" moments. That will only work a small number of times... if any. Be prepared to establish a way to follow up with the information you have discussed. Be aware that the decision process will be longer and drawn out. The Analyst may also want to speak to a trusted peer who is using the product. Anecdotal evidence will not be a great proof source in this situation.

- The **Enthusiast** will be hard to keep on track. This is the person who has his favorite sports team plastered on the wall and maybe even a picture with his idol. He may be the surgeon for the local college hockey or football team and he will want to talk about everything but business. By the time you know it, you are being ushered out and haven't even gotten close to a discussion about Features and Benefits, let alone uncovered a need that he or she may have. It's going to be a challenge for you if you are the same personality type, and even more difficult if you are a Moderator. If you have a driven personality like a Dominator, you may become impatient and risk the chance of not being invited back. Try to keep the outside discussions not relevant to business upfront, and at certain intervals inject the key points you wanted to share. Planning for this call is going to be important so you have both a strategy for listening and a strategy for uncovering the right issues and needs... in-between the Monday Night Football highlights.

- The **Moderator** will give you all the time in the world and in fact may make you late for your next appointment. Be aware that a yes may not be a yes. They may be trying to appease you, even if they don't actually agree with what you are presenting. Be aware of their pace and adjust to it. If they want to spend time in a certain area, make sure you listen well, stay engaged, and respond thoughtfully. The exchange of dialogue is important with a Moderator, and a good Introduction will put them at ease and set the stage for a meaningful Discussion—the place where you build trust and rapport. Being a good listener with a Moderator is important and will allow the process to flow that much better.

SUMMARY

- The Introduction is the crucial space that allows you to find common ground. It will determine whether you will have a few seconds or several minutes.

- The process doesn't need to be canned or packaged.

- You must build rapport.

- Look for clues and be a detective when it comes to understanding your customer's personality style.

- Adapt to your customer's style quickly.

CHAPTER 12

TRANSITION ZONES AND BEYOND

A transition zone is the point in any selling situation where you move between one step in the process to another. Transitions can be seamless, or awkward. They might even stall the meeting completely, and that's as far as you will ever get. Most sales process training defines each step and details what happens during that step. This can make a presentation appear canned. While structure is helpful, rather than thinking, "Okay, now I'm in the Discussion," or "Now, I am Validating my product," the natural flow of conversation should be most important. Anytime the mechanics of a sales process become obvious, we run the risk of making the customer feel like they are being sold to... and as you know, no one likes to be sold to.

Sometimes in the transition zone there may be more dead space than you are comfortable with, because we always feel like we need to fill space with words. The hardest thing to do in a conversation is to not say anything. When you get good at transitioning though, a natural well-placed pause can have a lot of meaning.

Transitioning to the Discussion phase is probably the easiest. When you have done everything in the prior step to justify moving forward, you'll find the least resistance. In a transition from Intro to Discussion, your choice of words will vary depending on the personality type of your customer.

If you are a Dominator and speaking with an Analyst, you might again say that you appreciate the opportunity to discuss whatever topic you were there for, and that you wanted to take just a few minutes to ask relevant questions to gain insight. "I'd like to ask about your practice, what your patient population looks like, and see if there is a way I can add value to you and your patients."

Your choice of words will vary depending on the customer's personality type.

At that point, whatever personality type you are dealing with may say, "Well, I only have a few minutes," or "I'm happy with what I'm using," or something else that puts up a temporary stop sign. These initial roadblocks are normal, issuing ground rules for interaction in their space, and maybe even the first initial objections. But if you understand the personality type of your customer and adapt quickly, your Transitions will become seamless.

Do not try to hurry. You may want desperately to get out of the area known as *silence* or *dead air* as quickly as possible. We don't usually like to wait more than a few seconds for a response, so we respond entirely too quickly.

Key points to watch for and do in a Transition zone:

- Make sure you know your customer's communication style.

- Ask for permission to go to the next step. This permission to ask a few questions drops you right into the Discussion.

- Ask questions that will get you into the next step.

- Don't be in a rush. Pause before you speak.

In a Transition zone, you are simply moving from one step in the process to the next. To do that within each step may look something like this:

- **Introduction to Discussion**. "I appreciate your time today and I would just like to ask you a few questions to learn a little more about you and your practice."

- **Discussion to Feature Benefits**. In this transition you are gaining affirmation that you are addressing the right need. "If I understand you correctly..." then restate the need back to the customer.

  Once you have done that, the transition can be to Product, but not until then. Do not be too quick to get into Product. Maybe it's the clinical data around the product first, and then once you have gained interest, then circle back to the Benefits and then the Features that address the need. This is like Validating your product in reverse.

- **Feature/Benefit to Validation**. This transition should be almost natural because once you have made claims, the customer will look for a way to confirm that what you're saying is true.

  Remember a Benefit will make a claim about your product's Feature that will address the identified need. This is where you would traditionally present your supporting data. You can get there by restating the Feature/Benefit and demonstrating the validity of the claim through one or more credible sources. If it is a study, for example, then you should state who performed the study, where it was done, what the cohort size was, whether it was conducted using multiple centers, and what the outcome was.

- **Validation to Close**. The transition from Validation to Close, in a perfect world, should begin with summarizing the Features of a product that benefit whatever need has been established. The Benefit stakes a claim to a product feature that satisfies a need or solves an issue or a problem. If a Benefit has the potential to satisfy the need, then it must be Validated and your transition to a Close must begin by restating the benefit and the supporting material that validates it—a study, clinical history, even anecdotal support such as hundreds of people using the product, maybe even people they know.

For instance, "We talked about two major points (state the features) that could have a positive effect on outcomes by giving your patients better range of motion (the benefit). The studies we discussed from (studies) show a marked improvement at eighteen months (the validation)." Then the transition begins. "Is there anything else you would like to see in the way of supporting data?" If the response is no, then you can begin asking Closing questions. You have earned the right at this point. "Can I check your schedule to see what would be a good time to review the instruments?" Another way to transition might be: "Once we set up a time to review the instruments, can we add some cases?"

THE DISCUSSION

Some people will want to call this the *interview,* but again, the word *discussion* seems more interactive to me... less like an interrogation. When you transition to the Discussion and the tone is conversational, the process will feel seamless for your customer. The goal of the Discussion is to help the customer realize a need or problem that your product will help solve.

Critical information that will assist in making the Discussion go well would have been discovered during the Introduction. There you will have determined how much time you have, allowing you to structure your questions in a way that is productive and fits the allotted time frame.

Sometimes you may not even get through the Discussion phase, and that's okay. It's most important that you remain aware of what's going on in the conversation. Your ability to read body language is equally important to anything you may ever say. If you have planned appropriately and have the roadmap in your mind, then you will know when it's time to end the conversation. I can tell you from experience that it's not a good feeling to be cut off or interrupted. If you sense you are running out of time, you are probably a minute or two behind when you should have been wrapping it up.

When you have command of the Discussion, are aware of your surroundings, and read the body language appropriately, then you will have gone a long way to appearing much more professional and knowledgeable to your customer. It also allows you to use the time to set up and confirm the next steps in the process.

I have transitioned into Discussion many different ways throughout my career. Sometimes I have found the conversation more formal. From experience, when you have not established a good rapport, this is when formality is most prominent. Sometimes the customer doesn't give you the opportunity to get too close. In addition, personality types like an Analyst or a Dominator will generally be more direct and formal. Someone who is an Enthusiast or a Moderator will allow you to speak more freely.

If you are a Dominator and fast-paced, speaking with a Moderator who is slower-paced or an Enthusiast who wants to engage in longer off-topic conversation may frustrate you. Your challenge is to adapt quickly by slowing yourself down and engaging in the conversation.

If you happen to be an Analyst and want to dive into the facts and supporting data, you will be challenged by someone who is a slower-paced Moderator. You will also be challenged by someone who is a Dominator because while they know they need the facts and supporting data, they may be too impatient to sit there while you methodically review it with them. In this case you will need to be able to condense your material, resorting to the important bullet points. You can allow the Dominator to validate it later if necessary, by leaving the right supporting material, however this is not optimal.

Adapting to personality styles is not always easy and you will not be able to connect with everyone, however it doesn't mean you won't be able to conduct business with that person. You will simply have the greatest challenge with personality types that are opposite to you. That's why I can't stress enough the importance of your ability to adapt.

In the Discussion, you are developing questions around potential benefits your product may have that can solve a potential need of the customer. In fact, during the course of the Discussion you may uncover a need the customer didn't realize they had or an issue they want to solve. This will help you realize the Features and Benefits that can address these needs so you can present them when you transition to the next step.

More things happen in the discussion than you may first realize. The rapport-building continues, *genuine interest* becomes apparent from both parties, and by asking well thought out questions you begin to gain the respect of your customer and demonstrate the depth of your *knowledge*.

Asking Good Questions

If you find yourself asking questions that can be easily answered by a yes or no, then your conversation will be brief. Instead ask questions that prompt a thoughtful response, allowing you to gain the information needed to later present only those Features and Benefits that address the need you have uncovered.

Instead of asking, "Do you like a (particular feature)?"—which will likely get you a simple yes or no answer—ask "What has been your experience with (that feature)?" Then you are more likely to hear useful commentary.

For example, instead of asking:

- Are there any issues you need to address?
- Are you satisfied with your current instruments?
- Do you have any challenges you face with regard to...?

Now you will know to ask:

- How do you address...?
- What is it about ... that you like?
- What are some of the challenges you face with regard to your instruments in the surgery center?

While you can certainly follow a yes or no answer with another question, posing an opening question that requires feedback will always give you more information. Each question should be designed to build on the previous answer so that ultimately you uncover a need or an issue to resolve. In some cases, you may not uncover anything right away, however, the better you get to know your customer, the greater the chance that you will eventually find a product Feature or Benefit that can address a particular need they have.

An example of digging deeper through follow-up questions might go like this:

- "What is it you like about your current knee instruments?"

    o   "They are very reproduceable."

- "What might be some of the challenges you face with regard to moving them to the ASC (same-day setting)?"

    o   "I wish there were fewer trays, a little more streamlined."

- "What exactly do you mean?"

    o   "We have limited space and we aren't yet efficient enough to do multiple cases."

In this short scenario you have now asked questions that allow you to understand your prospect's need for:

- Turning over the instruments quicker
- Doing more cases

If your product portfolio or your system has a solution for this, then you should already know what to talk about as you transition to the next step. This type of dialogue can be used for any type of product or service.

FEATURE/BENEFITS

Within the discussion lies a very important part of the sales process—features and benefits. If you had measured on a scale, you would find that new salespeople tip conversations heavily on features and benefits during a sales call. After all, as a new salesperson just completing your company training, you are armed with product knowledge that was recently drilled into your brain and it's waiting to come out!

The transition to Feature/Benefit begins within the Discussion. By first asking questions in a way that allows the customer to elaborate, you have been able uncover a need and discover which features and benefits of your product will best address that need.

For a new salesperson, the temptation is to do what I call a "feature/benefit dump," telling the customer everything you know about your product or service. Now you can rest easy, though. After having asked appropriate questions during the Discussion phase, all you now need to do is present only those features of your product that address this need, or which will benefit the customer in a way that completely resolves the need or issue.

An example of a feature and benefit in this case may look like:

- *Feature*: "We can cut your four trays down to one."
- *Benefit*: "This will minimize set-up time and decrease turnover time, so you can do two extra cases."

While this example may seem overly simplified, it is important to remember two things. First, ask the questions that will gain you feedback to uncover a customer need they would like to address or resolve. Then, armed with that information, present the features and benefits that will address that need.

You do not need to demonstrate features of your product which do not address the need you have uncovered. Avoid a "feature/benefit dump" at all costs!

KNOW YOUR PRODUCT. KNOWLEDGE IS POWER

My mom always used to joke, "Gerry, you're a jack of all trades and a master of none." I guess there are a couple of ways you can look at that. When I was younger I wanted to be everything and try everything. I wanted to fly planes, I wanted to ride horses, I wanted to teach, and I always wanted to be the best at everything I did. But at some point, unless you dedicate yourself to a task 100%, it's unlikely you will rise to the top. I mention all of this, not because it's a bad thing, but to the contrary, I believe you should learn everything you can—as that great philosopher Mom also said: *"Anything you learn is not lost."*

In sales, I really believe the more you know about many different topics, the better. Let's face it, we are self-promoters and that's a good thing, but it doesn't mean you have to act like you know things you don't. In conversation and while you are finding common ground with a customer or prospect, you will come across as knowledgeable and well-rounded as long as you are honest, humble, and continue to show *genuine interest* in the other person.

One of the biggest favors you can do for yourself is to become a student of your product and your industry. Beyond that, knowing your competition's product is equally important, as well as knowing all of the related factors that can affect your customer. In orthopedics, I have seen the changes within the industry that have had a profound effect on both our surgeon and healthcare professional customers as well as the companies that provide the products they use.

When you know your product, you can become a valuable resource to your primary customer and any supporting casts that need to know and understand what the product is and how it works.

I think you do need to be careful how you use your *knowledge*, however, because it can become a detriment instead of an asset very quickly. Even if you know it all… don't be a know-it-all. As a young sales representative, I used to attend countless hip and knee surgeries weekly, as well as trauma cases where the surgeon would be using plates and screws or an intramedullary rod to repair a fracture. At first, as much as I studied the technique and the procedure, I would be nervous because almost undoubtedly someone—even the surgeon—was going to ask a question about a certain size or something in general about the procedure. What I learned is that I needed to be mindful and present my knowledge only at the appropriate time and in such a way that it came across as helpful and not pontificating.

Product knowledge is something that can't be taken lightly. You can only get so many passes with "I don't know but I'll find out for you." Whether it is presenting Features and Benefits during a sales call or being available as a resource when the product is being used, you must position yourself as just that… a resource, a student of your industry, someone who never oversteps their bounds by inferring or giving the impression that you know more than you do.

I learned to become a resource to my surgeon customers and operating room staff by doing middle of the night trauma cases, usually with an on-call staff who didn't know where all of the orthopedic instruments were located on the shelf if they needed something in a hurry. But I did know their placement and I would inconspicuously guide them and the scrubbed-in techs so that each case would go smoothly. I never drew attention to myself, but that didn't matter to me. I knew when I did a good job and felt very satisfied driving home at the end of a day because of it.

Back in 1997, I was in on a case with two surgeons who were partners. It was a complicated total knee revision and quite frankly, at the time, I had only been in on a handful of revision cases. I studied hard and long beforehand and I knew everything I needed to know to get through the case.

At very critical times during the procedure when certain bone cuts needed to be made, I knew which jigs/cut guides should be used to prepare for the correct augments and what steps needed to be taken in order to achieve the best outcome. At one point the assisting surgeon blurted out that I was wrong about a certain step. I calmly stood my ground and explained why. The lead surgeon said, "Makes sense," and just went with it without even acknowledging the other surgeon.

When the case was over, I remember walking several steps behind the lead surgeon down the hall. All of a sudden he stopped, turned, and waited for me. "Gerry, thank you! You were right on the money with that," he said, referring to the other surgeon's disagreement, "and you did an incredible job in there." It was at that very point that I realized how critical it is to know everything about your product and how it works. If you are a true resource, the accolades will come in ways you never imagined.

Whatever your business or industry, word travels fast. The world is much smaller than we believe on any given day. If you strive to be the best you can be—and in many cases grow through baptism under fire—your rewards will come. They will come in the way of earned respect that will, without a doubt, translate into opportunity after opportunity.

Strive to be the best under fire... and the rewards will come!

Stay humble in the process. Stay humble, but with pride. Let the competition boast, but know you can surpass them with respect gained by using the Pillar of *knowledge* wisely.

Summary

- A *transition zone* is the point in any selling situation where you move between one step in the process to another.

- If you know the personality type of your customer and adapt quickly, the transition becomes seamless.

- When you transition to the Discussion and the tone is conversational, it all seems effortless.

- The goal of the Discussion is to help the customer realize a need or problem that your product will help solve.

- Become a student of your product and your industry. When you know your product, you can become a resource.

- Let the competition boast, but you can surpass them with the respect you gain by using your *knowledge* wisely.

CHAPTER 13

VALIDATION

Validation consists of all the information that substantiates any benefit claim you make about your product. In a feature/benefit presentation, you will make claims, however unsubstantiated or unvalidated claims will cause objections that you won't be able to resolve.

Each of the Four Pillars will serve you well when it comes to validating your product. Especially when it comes to *knowledge*. Validating your product in such a way that presents facts supporting your benefit claim shows that you have been honest in your assessment of their needs, have sought to do the right thing for them (*integrity*), and have shown *genuine interest* in a positive outcome.

The information you possess to Validate your product doesn't change, but the extent that you deliver it will vary depending on your customer's style. In other words, you will validate the claims made in the feature/benefit presentation based solely on the needs you uncover in the Discussion.

Validation—and how you deliver it—will make all the difference when you get to a place where you are ready to Close or ask for a commitment.

ANALYST

If you are speaking with an Analyst then you not only need to have command of all the facts but be ready to discuss and deliver them in detail. "I don't know, I'll get back to you" will never get you to the Close with an Analyst. If your company has technical briefs to support claims and perhaps summarize a key clinical paper, make sure you study them. Make notes on your own copy and know it to the point you can accurately cite the critical information.

DOMINATOR

A Dominator is not going to give you the time to recite *War and Peace* to validate your claims, but you still need to get the information out there. Remember the Dominator is fast-paced so your challenge is to disseminate the info in snippets at the right time during the conversation.

The key with a Dominator—as with any relationship—is trust. If you have done a good job at developing rapport and building trust in a new relationship, then you will be in a good place when it comes time to validate your claims.

Most of the time, the cliff notes version of validating your claims will suffice. Then leave the information with your customer afterward, perhaps putting little sticky notes on the document with a few words describing what you want the customer to pay attention to. Dominators are good at getting the information they need to make a decision by listening to those they trust, as well as doing their own research.

ENTHUSIAST

Remember our Enthusiast is tough to keep focused, so this is another challenge you will face in the delivery of information that validates your claims. You already know the conversation will have a tendency to wander, so be prepared to cite short bursts of facts in only the area that will Validate the key benefits you presented in the Discussion.

Peter Falk played the character of Columbo in a well-known TV series during the '70s. Columbo always appeared a bit disheveled, however he had a great way of adapting to whatever personality style he was communicating with. In fact, once the person he was speaking with thought they were finished, he had a very non-threatening way of coming back and saying, "Oh, one more thing," followed by a question. So if an Enthusiast is off track you may get the chance to use your best Columbo impression and say, "Oh by the way, one more thing," and then ask a question that brings them back on track to the Conclusion of your conversation by leaving them with your final thought.

MODERATOR

The Moderator is going to give you time. I recommend you use it wisely. If you have a lot of time, you can get into trouble. Have you ever heard of anyone talking themselves out of a sale? This personality type is where you can stumble into this issue. The Moderator will want certainty. We all want certainty, but a Moderator even more so.

Remember, it's "I like you" and "you like me" with a Moderator. I find myself circling back to make sure I haven't missed something in identifying a need. Sometimes a Moderator will not throw the objection up so you can hit it out of the park; they are the king of curve balls. Right up through Validation it will seem like everything is going great. However, when you get to a Close, you will begin to uncover underlying objections. Make sure you have not cut any corners at all with a Moderator. Validation is key.

SUMMARY

- Validation is key to you getting to a successful sale. Unsubstantiated claims will be challenged and rebuked.

- The Analyst and the Dominator will most likely challenge you directly while the Enthusiast and the Moderator won't tell you what they are thinking. You could walk away high-fiving and not even realize you lost a sale.

- Validation depends on trust. If you are speaking with any of the other personality types, you may not have to go into the detail an Analyst expects. You should always have the information available but you may only be able to deliver an abbreviated version. With the Dominator, again just plan on the cliff note version almost all the time. The Enthusiast won't remember half of what you say, but the Moderator will listen closely yet be looking for reasons to trust you as you Validate your product.

- Validating can be as easy as referencing the data that backs up the claim, or making a call with another customer who is already using your product. Be aware of your customer's personality style, and as always, be prepared to Validate in a way they will be able to receive your information and that it will make sense.

CHAPTER 14

HANDLING OBJECTIONS

Objections surface when you begin to ask for a commitment. It could be a commitment to buy, or simply a commitment to go to the next step in the process. This is the place where salespeople tend to fall apart. In fact, most salespeople, especially early in their careers, tend to take objections personally. Remember though, the customer is most likely not objecting or rejecting *you*, they are objecting to something about your product.

This is why it is absolutely critical that you ask the right questions in the early part of a Discussion so that you uncover the right need. If you do not uncover the right need, everything that follows will lead up to only one thing—an objection.

Objections are good though, because that means you are still on the playing field. At least now you have a chance to solve it.

How do you solve an objection?

- The first step is to reconfirm that you are solving the right problem or issue.

In other words, did you uncover a need that the customer has and wants to solve?

- You will need to go back and restate the Benefit of your product and Validate, but if you didn't uncover the right need then you are going to validate something the customer doesn't really care about.

- Restate the objection and if the customer agrees that is correct, you can then begin to transition back.

- As you are restating Benefits, ask if this was important and also if there was anything that was missed.

The following dialogue is an example of steps needed when transitioning back to uncover the real objection. It is only a static representation and will vary depending on the customer and your own personalized delivery.

For example, the customer might say, "Your instruments look more cumbersome than what I am used to." So you might respond, "I understand the instrumentation seems a little more cumbersome than what you have been working with. Is it all of the instruments or a specific one or two?"

Perhaps the customer answers, "Just this one here." Then you can say, "Okay, got it. Just to reconfirm, one of the things you mentioned when we first started talking was the overall design of the implant and how you liked the anterior flange which you thought would potentially alleviate some anterior knee pain."

"Yes, I agree," the customer might say, "but I'm not going to sacrifice my streamlined instruments. It hasn't been that big an issue."

Objections are good, because that means you are still on the playing field.

Perhaps something else has surfaced. Maybe it wasn't so much the anterior knee pain issue as it was the time involved in doing the case.

You might follow up with, "So if I understand you correctly, the anterior knee pain would be nice to totally eliminate, but you really like your instruments. Is that because it allows you to do the case faster?"

"Why yes, of course. I would like to do at least two more cases a day." Now you're starting to uncover something. You might say, "I see that is important, especially if you are busy enough.

So let me ask you a couple questions... do you like the design of our implant?"

You get a quick yes, so perhaps you suggest, "If I could streamline the instruments and get you a jig similar to this one you like, would you want to do a series?"

Another yes... though there's usually a "but" waiting in the wings. "But I would want to do a lab first..." or "I told you I like your design and the story behind your company but..." or "Time is at a premium."

The dialogue here is common. You think you did all of the pre-work in the Discussion, but you missed the fact that while this customer was having knee pain issues with his current system, he liked the effectiveness of the instrumentation. While you did uncover a need, you may have been solving a problem that was not one he felt compelled to solve immediately. What happened instead is that when you transitioned back, you found that the primary concern was the instruments and doing the case faster and doing more cases. The knee pain is a nice thing to alleviate but you were not going to get the sale on that point alone.

Make no mistake... you are always going to get objections. They will just be more difficult if you didn't uncover the right need first. This example could have concluded many ways but the salesperson did use the process to his benefit which helped him get back on track.

When objections pop up, welcome them. It's like the prospective customer saying, "I may want to buy from you but you haven't helped me discover why just yet."

The adage, "The only dumb questions are the ones you don't ask," applies here. Begin by restating the objection. Transition back to the Benefit discussion and make sure the benefit is addressing the correct need.

Did you uncover an issue that needs to be addressed and solved? As in the example above, the real need may only surface later, and that's okay. That other earlier need may be secondary, but it might help you as long as you face the most imminent need head-on and solve it as well.

SUMMARY

- Welcome objections! It sounds crazy but if you can get to the point where you welcome objections, your confidence is going to increase tenfold.

- Objections are likely to surface when you ask for a commitment. It could be a commitment to buy, but also as simple as moving to the next step in the process. Trust in yourself and trust in the process.

- Restate the objection clearly, then restate the benefit and gain agreement, but then don't be afraid to ask if you have missed something. Sometimes customers will not initially share all the information needed in order to help them. It may take more than one time transitioning back, and it will not always happen in one meeting.

- Remember, if you get an objection, you are on the playing field. I don't know about you, but I would much rather be on the field than sitting on the bench.

CHAPTER 15

CLOSE

The word *close* implies that you are done with something, so maybe that's not the right word. When you think about it, when speaking about an order or a tangible product, "closed" business is actually just the beginning—the beginning of a new relationship, and the beginning of more needs yet to fill.

When you do begin to bring a sales call to a conclusion you will be asking for a commitment. It may be a commitment to use your product or it could be simply the next step in the process.

If you have done everything in the process and not shorted yourself or your customer, then you are less likely to get an objection, though if you do, it will not be so strong that it can't be overcome. If you have done everything in the process and the objection surfaces, it is positive.

TRIAL CLOSE (AFFIRMATIONS)

When you ask for affirmation anytime during the process, you are testing the waters. This is often referred to as a "trial close" and is sometimes reassuring at the right times because it will at least give you some assurance that you are on the right path.

Some sales programs say, "Close early and often." But what does this mean? At its face value, your customers will see this coming a mile away. Be careful how you approach this and don't overuse "if I" or "if then, would you" type of questions. Not that you should never use them at all, but just remember... no one wants to be sold anything, so if possible, I try to use *trial closing* in the form of affirmations by the customer, such as "Are we in agreement?" or "Do we both agree?"

Asking "Do you understand?" can be a *trial close* and you are simply both acknowledging that you agree. You can't move on unless you both agree, and in doing so, this allows you to move forward in the process.

Reaffirming an affirmation by your customer is just another building block along the way to confirming you:

- have uncovered an issue that needs to be solved.
- haven't missed anything along the way.

When someone tells me they like a certain feature of my product, I generally follow it up with a question like "What about it do you like?" or "What issue does it address for you?"

You are going to get two things back: The first is the affirmation or answer you would want in a *trial close* when it's ready to move to the next step in the process. Second, you find out whether you have uncovered the correct need.

When you think about it, if someone hasn't acknowledged or agreed to something, how would you expect to move forward? At any point, if you get an objection from any personality type during a *trial close*, or simply that the customer doesn't affirm, then you should be prepared to transition back to the previous step.

If you have received positive affirmations and acknowledgments throughout the process and your customer is giving you all the right feedback, then you have earned the right to Close, but I would like to say something even stronger than that... you have earned the right to go to the next step in the *relationship*.

When you transition from Validation to Close, start by summarizing briefly.

This will vary depending on the personality type you are speaking with. An Analyst will be more in-depth and detailed. A Dominator will be the cliff notes again. For an Enthusiast, you may want to repeat just two of the most important points, and for a Moderator you will want to restate the next steps and again make sure they are okay with whatever that step is.

WHAT DOES CLOSING NEW BUSINESS MEAN?

The keys to closing new business are:

- Going through the process and not missing any steps.
- Trusting in yourself and the process.
- Putting your customer first.
- Asking for a commitment.

I have been on more sales calls than I can count as a sales representative and as a regional manager and as a VP of Sales. Sometimes I let the salesperson handle the call and just observed with little input.

When a salesperson does not follow the process it is evident. They have not taken the time to adapt to the personality style of their customer, never transitioned to a Discussion, and launched head-on into what I have referred to as the "feature/benefit dump." This acts as a crutch for the salesperson who has not followed the process. He/she has not made a good transition into the Discussion and just used the product as a feature/benefit Discussion. Remember, you should never be talking about features and benefits unless you are doing it to demonstrate a feature that has a benefit which will solve a problem or issue, or fill a need.

The salesperson who fails to follow steps will resort to phrases like "Give me a shot." What does that mean? It's code for "I have no idea what your needs are, but hey, I'm a good guy, so please, please use my product."

This will not be you though, because you now have the tools that will allow you to help your customer, fill a need, and solve potential problems, both now and in the future. Asking for business is only a right if you have entered a place where it is mutually beneficial.

An example of a Close could look something like this:

> "I appreciate you taking the time today. I am looking forward to working with you. We talked about a lot of things, including the instrument change you would want. It also sounds like you were very pleased with the design as it relates to lower stress and potential for less anterior knee pain. Have we missed anything? I'll set up an appointment on the way out to review the changes and look forward to seeing you in the next few weeks. If you can think of anything else please call me anytime."

The example is just that... an example. Nothing should feel canned. If it feels canned to you, it will feel canned to your customer. You should say these things in your own words. When you speak in a way that uses your own words and mannerisms, you will come across with authenticity. When you come across as authentic, you also show *genuine interest*, and that will be reflected back to you in your customer's response.

Strong relationships, like old buildings, are built on a solid foundation.

Strong relationships, like old buildings, are built on a solid foundation. The Pillars that your relationships should rest firmly on are *honesty, integrity, knowledge,* and *genuine interest*. These supports will surface throughout the process and are never so evident than in the closing of new business.

SUMMARY

- The *trial close* is nothing more than an affirmation by your customer acknowledging that you are on the right path. It allows you to move on in the process.

- A Close will ask for commitment. If you have missed something in the process, expect to hear an objection.

The severity of the objection is going to vary
on the need you identified and whether tl
being adequately filled. If you didn't properl
need, you can get lured into a "feature/benef
and when the objection comes, you won't be able to solve
it.

- When you have developed trust, adjusted to your customer's personality style, and successfully Validated information around a correctly identified need, then the Close will be a natural progression. In your own words, it will come across as authentic and not contrived.

- Don't think of a Close as something that builds. Instead, think of it as a natural progression in the process of developing new business and a new relationship.

PART FOUR

The Challenges

CHAPTER 16

SALES CALL RELUCTANCE

"The only thing we have to fear is fear itself."
~Franklin D. Roosevelt

George W. Dudley and Shannon L. Goodson, in their book *The Psychology of Sales Call Reluctance,* define call reluctance as:

> "...a career-threatening condition which limits what salespeople achieve by emotionally limiting the number of sales calls they make. Some have trouble using the phone as a prospecting tool. Others have trouble initiating face-to-face contact with prospective buyers. Many have trouble doing both."

While not everyone feels call reluctance, the majority may be predisposed to some form of it. Dudley and Goodson go on to say that 80% of the salespeople who fail in the first year do so because of insufficient prospecting activities.

Your belief in sales is either one of your biggest assets or your greatest nemesis.

Sales call reluctance is real. I have seen it time and again in others, and I have experienced it myself. Driving hours from Maine to New Hampshire yet not going into the surgeon's office was a perfect example. It stemmed from many things that I have since overcome, but like an addiction, I must keep it in check all the time.

I was 24 years old and just off active duty in the Marine Corps. I had been beaten down at Paris Island and rebuilt as a Marine who took orders and did what he was told. Fortunately for me, the one thing that aided me most was a never-quit attitude, but what are the causes of this potential career killer?

THE ROOT CAUSES OF SALES CALL RELUCTANCE

Belief in Sales

Your belief in sales is either one of your biggest assets or your greatest nemesis when it comes to committing to the activities that will make you successful. If you believe at your core that sales is somehow not an honorable profession, then you won't even feel comfortable with the word "salesman," "sales representative," or anything else with *sales* in your job title.

Fear of Rejection

Fear of rejection is a common thing in life. If you are rejected enough times, you may start feeling beat up. Negative thoughts will begin to manifest. You may ask yourself, "Why does this always happen to me?"

No one likes the feeling of being rejected, and because of that, it becomes easier to create alternate avenues to keep busy so you won't have to experience that gut-wrenching feeling. The only problem with the other activities (busy work) is that they don't generate sales.

> **Procrastination is an avoidance mechanism designed to keep you from experiencing sales call reluctance.**

Lack of Knowledge or Preparation

If you feel that your customer has more knowledge than you do about your product, or in my case of medical device sales, that your customer has more knowledge in general about the procedure, this can create a large amount of anxiety. It goes hand in hand with the lack of preparation. If you are not prepared, you will experience anxiety over not being able to answer all the questions or appearing less than knowledgeable.

SYMPTOMS OF SALES CALL RELUCTANCE

The symptoms of sales call reluctance stem from its root causes. If you are a salesperson, you know in your heart if you are reluctant to make sales calls. You may also have an idea what the root cause is. If you are a manager, the symptoms mentioned next should give you clues that will help identify root causes so you can help your sales staff.

Procrastination

Have you ever procrastinated before? Why? Most likely it's because of something you didn't want to do, or you didn't want to confront. Procrastination in sales call reluctance is an avoidance mechanism. It's a failure to prepare, or preparing at the last minute.

It could also be the result of an abundance of preparation, however, so much so that you keep putting off an appointment or presentation.

Procrastination can take many forms, but it is an avoidance mechanism designed to keep you from experiencing sales call reluctance.

Over-Preparation

Some would say that you can never over-prepare, and I think that is true, however over-preparation in relation to sales call reluctance is preparing to make a call that you may never make. You can keep busy by preparing all day long and you can even convince yourself that you have had a very productive day, but you won't overcome procrastination unless you overcome the root cause of sales call reluctance.

Lack of Leads in Your Pipeline

Not having an adequate number of new leads in your pipeline is a sign of call reluctance. Sure, you can write down any name you want, but ultimately unless you make contact and begin working through a process, nothing happens. Another sign associated with this symptom is calling on previous customers. These are usually your good accounts where you have easy access and they are happy to see you. These are the *milk runs* we talked about in Chapter 11.

OVERCOMING SALES CALL RELUCTANCE

Sales call reluctance in my past came in many variations. It ganged up on me in my mind to the point that it emotionally prevented me from making the necessary amount of cold calls I needed to become successful.

In those days we didn't have iPhones and texting didn't exist as a crutch. I had developed a fear of rejection after being denied appointments. I didn't realize that with cold calling, I would need to make several attempts before I might even get an appointment.

What else did I fear? Looking back now and analyzing it, I didn't believe that anyone liked salespeople, especially the people we call the "gatekeepers"... the secretary or administrative assistant, guarding the door to the back office.

I believe now that call reluctance goes right back to your belief in selling. This belief will ultimately dictate what your commitment to action will become. If you believe that sales is an honorable profession, if you believe in your product, if you believe in yourself, and you believe in your abilities, then you will at least be in a place where you can commit to taking the action steps necessary to become successful. Beyond that, it goes back to your goals and how much you really want something.

One of the things I have found throughout my career is that when I felt low, when I felt rejected, and when I felt all alone— usually at some rest area on a drive to somewhere to make a sales call—is that once I did the first call—making some sort of contact, even if it wasn't the best call in the world—my confidence was boosted and I used that to build on and make the next call and the next.

If you are on a roll now and things are clicking, use that to your advantage. Don't get complacent. Make as many calls as you can. Use the confidence you have gained from a volley of successes to build on it. Success breeds success.

STEPS TO OVERCOMING SALES CALL RELUCTANCE

Let's go back to a few of the root causes for a moment:

- Belief in selling
- Fear of rejection
- Lack of knowledge or preparation

Belief in selling goes back to something that may be tucked away in your subconscious. Do you believe selling is a less than honorable profession? Are you afraid to have the word "sales" associated with your name? What is it that you tell your friends and family that you do?

If that's the case, how do you turn that around? How can you feel good about what you are doing in your career to the point you want to tell someone, "I'm in sales," or "I'm in orthopedic sales," or "I'm in spine sales," or whatever it is?

Ask yourself these questions:

- How is my product helping my customers?
- What problems am I solving for my customers?
- What valuable service do I provide to my customers?
- What difference am I making in the lives of the people my products are helping?

Work with me here. I'm showing you this because I want you to be able to raise your standards. You should come to know how valuable you are to your customers and your company. In the medical device world, you can say:

- "My products are helping surgeons perform surgery in less time with better results."

- "My products are helping patients return to normal activities."

- "My knowledge provides a valuable resource to my surgeons and support staff. They know I am a valuable resource for their team."

- "What I do daily, along with the products and service I provide, makes a real difference in my customers' lives and the lives they touch."

Write these statements down or take a picture of them with your phone. Keep them with you and refer to them on a regular basis—especially when you're not having your best day—to remind you of who you are and why you do what you do, and why you are proud of what you do.

I know this sounds like positive self-talk, but if you have been filling your runaway computer (aka your brain) with negative self-talk, why let it win? Fill your head with so much good stuff that you begin to believe in yourself, your profession, and the difference you are making in people's lives.

---

*"Our only limitations are those we
set up in our own minds"* ~Napoleon Hill

One of the things that may help you is taking the time to relive a positive event in your mind from start to finish. Do you remember the colonel who spent all those years in captivity and played his best round of golf because he had played the course over and over in his mind? Visualization can help you do the same thing.

I suggest you think about a sales call that went well for you. Remember everything about it from start to finish. You just need to reinforce the victory in your mind. If you have done it before, you can do it again. Focus on that success rather than the what-ifs. You have no control over the what-ifs.

If you are fairly new to sales and are experiencing call reluctance—which if you are honest, stems from a negative belief in yourself or your abilities—then use another life experience to bridge the gap.

In the past you have done something extremely hard that made you proud when you finally completed it. Draw on that mental image, and visualize your future success.

In years past, I told myself that because I made it through Paris Island and Marine Corps boot camp, I could do anything. When times get tough, I tell myself this is nothing compared to the corps. You can accomplish the same, and as you accumulate more and more victories in your sales career, you will be able to call on them in your memory to lift you over the top when you are feeling challenged by the next cold call or presentation, or a difficult case where the staff needs your expertise.

FEAR OF REJECTION: OVERCOMING THE SILENT KILLER

If you have a fear of rejection, why do you think that is? It's because rejection hurts, and with enough of it, your brain decides that enough is enough. Let's face it, rejection can be a silent killer; it can eat you up inside… but only if you let it.

When your belief in your abilities is aligned with your belief in selling, the fear of rejection will diminish.

When your belief in yourself and your abilities is in alignment with your belief in selling, the fear of rejection will diminish. It may never completely go away though, and it may later surface through feelings like:

159

- "What if I mess up my presentation?"
- "What if they don't like me?"
- "How can I ever compete against their current rep?"
- "This customer is so much older and wiser than me."

Just like we talked about visualizing success in order to create a good outcome, you can also use visualization to overcome the fear of rejection. The fear begins when you catch yourself asking bad questions and manifesting the outcome of those questions to paint a negative picture. Once you paint that negative picture, you begin to feel that negative outcome just as if it were real. Your mind won't know the difference between what is real and what is not.

When you find yourself in a negative self-talk, stop! Put down that paint brush, start with a white canvas, and paint the picture we talked about earlier.

You now have the skill level to customize your presentations to identify needs based on questions which you execute effectively because you understand your customer's personality style. You have a much better chance of developing a rapport with that individual, so yes, they will probably like you more. When it comes right down to it, you will have earned their respect.

A WORD ABOUT RELATIONSHIPS

Some relationships are like blood, thicker than water, but a client may not give you all their business just because of that. Think about that the next time you question your profession. A customer who values the relationship with a rep so much that it factors in the equation to convert business should tell you how much the industry values its sales representatives. That's actually something you should feel good about. And by the way, you will be in that same position someday too, when you develop relationships that foster loyalty.

You can't worry about the customer's relationship with their sales rep. Yes, you should be aware of it and respect it, but in my experience, no one company can provide the perfect solution for everything and everyone.

In addition, some sales reps get complacent and assume their customer will never switch or try something new. That's why you can't make assumptions. Don't deliver a halfhearted presentation or go through a sales call with anything less than your best, simply because you have talked yourself into believing a relationship with another rep or company is too strong. When you follow the process, you may uncover a need that the customer didn't know existed, and in doing so, you may find a pathway to work together. Don't worry about the other sales rep; worry about always doing your best and not short-cutting the process.

AGE AND EXPERIENCE

When I was a young salesman, it seemed like every customer was older than me. I really let that get to me. I assumed that because they were older, I couldn't possibly help them. At the time they were my parents' age and I had grown up respecting my parents. Other sales representatives had more experience and more in common with the customers than I did. This one factor created more symptoms of call reluctance for me that contributed to my fear of being rejected.

I had less education at the time and didn't think I was worthy to be on the same playing field. In orthopedics and the medical device industry, clinical knowledge is a key component for walking the walk and talking the talk. I couldn't do either because I hadn't seen enough surgeries. I wanted to learn, I had the desire, but I believed my lack of knowledge prevented me from having much more than feature/benefit conversations. It was a limiting belief that could have squashed my career in the first year.

You are probably wondering how I overcame this. For starters, I never pretended to know more than I did, and I always demonstrated a willingness to learn. There were a few surgeon customers for whom I had a great deal of respect, and I will never forget the one who took me under his wing. While I never did much business with him, he would teach me things and answer questions for me so that I would begin to understand and gain confidence.

The customer I mentioned from those early days in Northern Maine, was one of the few customers using my products. I was at his account most every Monday and Thursday and I watched and learned as he performed surgery after surgery. He also took me under his wing, and it wasn't long before I was speaking with more authority and could hold my own in most clinical and technical conversations.

Experience is also the counter-balance to any of your worries related to age. One way you can overcome the knowledge factor—if that is a major contributor to your call reluctance—is to go into different regions and observe cases and sales calls. Ask to follow an experienced representative and watch cases with him if that is part of his day. Watch how he interacts with his customers and ask the customers who are friendly to your rep and your company some of the questions you might not ask a customer in your own territory. Attend industry meetings, but don't hang out by the booth area if you are exhibiting. Instead, sit in the conference and take notes. If you have a question on a certain topic then ask someone following the break.

If you build your knowledge base, you will bridge the age and experience gap. Experience doesn't have an age number associated with it. My mother also said, *"Knowledge is power,"* and she was right again.

You will also find it easier to bridge the generation gap if you know something about where that person is from, where they went to school, and some of the things they like to do. In addition, your knowledge of current events will allow you access to many conversations.

SUMMARY

- Sales call reluctance is a career-threatening condition which limits what salespeople achieve by emotionally limiting the number of sales calls they make.

- Your belief in sales is either one of your biggest assets or your greatest nemesis when it comes to committing to the activities that will make you successful in sales.

- Fear of rejection is a common thing in life.

- If you are not prepared, you experience anxiety over not being able to answer all the questions or appear knowledgeable.

Sales call reluctance can be the silent killer in your career if you let it. There is no silver bullet or magic wand to wave that will rid you of it, but you will beat it if you follow some of the suggestions brought up here.

If this is something you struggle with, I suggest reading *The Psychology of Sales Call Reluctance,* by George W. Dudley and Shannon L. Goodson.

CHAPTER 17

CHALLENGES ARE A PART OF LIFE

You meet challenges every day. Some are more critical than others, and some will test your resolve down to the very core of who you are. We never know how we will react when we meet challenges and adversity. We would like to think that we will never give in, but I don't believe we can really know until something faces us head-on.

In my career, I have always worked to get to the next level. Along the way, I may have lost my vision now and then. Life sometimes does a good job at getting us caught up. Complacency can be one of the most dangerous components to losing your drive and motivation, and abandoning your dreams.

A close friend encouraged me to write this section of the book because he believed so much in what I accomplished over the last few years and especially over a period of sixty days last year. This close friend used to be my fiercest competitor when we were both salesman for competing companies in the same territory. This person sometimes believed in me more than I believed in myself. I hope you have a friend like this somewhere along your journey.

Generally, when I get committed to doing something, I tell people about it so it becomes my own accountability tool. I never want to say I'm going to do something and then not do it. The stress and embarrassment would be too much for me to bear.

Last year, I reviewed goals I'd set back in 2008 and 2009. I had written down things like earning a bachelor's degree, getting my MBA, teaching, competing in equestrian events, and being a better husband and father. You name it, I put it all out there in my personal and professional goals, and because it was written down, I had held myself accountable. The good news was that I accomplished a lot of those things.

I believe now the danger of getting complacent in a position may cause you to be caught off-guard or unprepared should change happen unexpectedly within your company.

After his third week on the job, my new VP of Sales told me during a Friday afternoon phone conversation that we were on the same page about a lot of things—probably more than I realized. The following Tuesday, however, at an airport hotel, just 62 days before Christmas, he walked up and handed me a folder with a severance package. Until negotiated, that package extended only until December 23, just two days before Christmas.

The VP was clear that the severance was "without cause" and not for "performance." It was also clear in just my year and a half as East Regional Vice President, that my team and I had managed to return to growth and I had done a very good job.

Those of you in sales or sales management know that company agreements are structured so they can terminate you without cause. So as my new VP of Sales later said to others, "Let's just say when a new coach comes in, he brings his own players." I hold no ill will toward the company or him. He made his decision and he will be accountable to it however it turns out.

So began the challenges I alluded to earlier. At my age, I felt sure I would be up against younger candidates if I chose to enter a sales capacity or look for a regional manager position. For a few days I reflected on my life—what had been good and not so good. I questioned for a short time whether I had the fire in the belly for another fight, and then to keep climbing. Good Marines never die, they just live to take the hill. I was facing a job loss and some potentially serious personal issues at the same time. The stars had aligned all right, but I didn't care much for the order.

At the same time as my severance, the company also cancelled my hotel and reservations for the American Academy of Hip and Knee Surgeons. I recognized the situation I was in and I didn't like it. I had no other alternative but to acknowledge it. I investigated my options and then made my own decision.

That decision was simply to register for the meeting. I used my acquired air miles and hotel "points" to reach the meeting in Dallas. For an exhausting two days I walked the convention floor, meeting with more people than I can count.

I had brought my resumé with me and looked for opportunities. I never sold myself short. The funny thing is, once I made that decision, my confidence emerged. It was uncomfortable, to say the least, to be a man without a company for the first time in almost 30 years, but I still walked the floor with confidence. I was engaging, and I never once looked or felt like I was running scared.

One of the things I like to share with people in this business— or any business for that matter—is the importance of staying relevant. I often felt bad for the guys I saw walking convention floors at meetings, whether they had a job or not, but who would go from one booth to the next talking to old friends and acquaintances about the "old times" and who they knew, saying things like: "Remember when," and "Business isn't what it used to be."

I purposely stayed away from those conversations. I was a Marine on a mission. I decided before I went there that I was still relevant. Just a few days before, a highly regarded U.S. surgeon said to me, "Gerry, this industry needs you." So armed with that, I set out to interview companies that had potential opportunities for me. I decided too that I still had the ability to make a difference in this industry and I could add a tremendous amount of value to a company that was the right fit for me.

At this point I had moved so far beyond the termination from my previous company that my own internal drive and will-power would not let me stop. I had too much to offer, and I had not only remained relevant in my career, I had become a student of it and I had become a student of sales in general.

While walking the convention floor, I met a friend who had wanted to hire me as a sales rep in the northeast about 18 years prior. I gave him the one-minute overview and he immediately told me about an opportunity for a VP of Sales position for the U.S.—not a regional position. This was a company that I would later find out wanted to build out their own hip and knee product portfolio and their sales and distribution for the entire country.

After speaking with the recruiter the following week, I received a phone interview with the CEO. After over an hour on the phone he asked me to come to the office two weeks later to make a presentation to their board of directors about how I would get them to their goals. Three weeks after that—and having been narrowed from five final candidates to just me and one other person—I was offered the job... the week before Christmas. During this period I also received two other job offers but did not perceive either as a good fit.

Some people say the only sure thing in life is death and taxes. That may be true but what will hit you square in the face more than once in your career is adversity, and with adversity comes a challenge. The question is: "What will you do?" If you get hit, the most natural thing in the world is to cover up. After that, you can assess the damage, and then you get to decide what to do next.

As simple as it may sound, you have to *recognize* the challenge and its potential consequences. Then you must *acknowledge* it. Don't simply ignore it and hope it goes away. *Investigate* all the possible options, and then *decide* what action you are going to take. Conduct your own "*RAID*" effectively:

- Recognize
- Acknowledge
- Investigate
- Decide

Decision and action go hand in hand. Doing nothing is also a decision, but a decision with action will send you off in a stronger direction. It has worked for me, and my wish for you is that when you are faced with a challenge and adversity, you will answer the call and bring out everything you have to offer. You are relevant, and you have more to offer than you even realize. But until you begin to take the steps forward and trust in yourself, little happens.

CONCLUSION

I want to thank you for letting me be a part of your journey in sales, if only for a brief period of time. It has been a privilege to share my stories filled with success, failure, and experiences that have shaped my sales career and my life.

I hope you have found some things to take with you that will propel you to the next level in your career, help you attain your goals, effectively communicate with people you meet along the way, and give you the belief that if I can do it, you can certainly do it, too.

You and I are kindred spirits. You picked up a book because you wanted to get to the next level in your sales career. I hope you found that in your struggles, you are not alone. Others have trod the same path in search of the excellence you now pursue. In doing so, you have demonstrated that you too are a lifelong learner. In the words of Stephen Covey, "You seek to understand before being understood," and in so doing, you have increased your knowledge and understanding of people and the world of sales.

I also hope that we get a chance to meet along the way. I would love to shake your hand and hear the stories and experiences that have shaped your career.

ONE FINAL NOTE

In times of challenge and adversity, remember to surround yourself with quality friends. These are friends who will believe in you... not pity you. These are friends who will lift you up and remind you of who you really are. They will tell you what they see.

You will be better served by a kick in the pants from these friends than by dwelling with the misery-loves-company crowd.

Good quality friends will be there to nudge you along the way and to cheer you on, but it's up to you to pull yourself up by your own bootstraps.

Good Selling!

ACKNOWLEDGMENTS

My family: To Sandy, Lauren, Stephanie, and Natalie for putting up with all the travel, the time away, and the non-stop pace of sales, and for your unconditional love and belief in me. To Cheryl, Jen, Ellen, and John for your undying faith and encouragement.

Mike Campbell: Through thick and thin, trusted friend since the fifth grade. Your friendship and trust have never wavered.

Steve Huff, Dover, New Hampshire: A friendship that seemed so unlikely. I'm honored to call you friend. You continue to push me and keep me believing in myself and how much life has to offer.

Steve deBree, Portland, Maine: For your thirty-four years of friendship, wisdom, knowledge, and expertise in sales.

Andy Kalajian, Alpharetta, Georgia (The Ragin Kalajian): The eternal optimist, your cup is half full attitude, and thirst for life and knowledge is something we could all learn from.

Mary Jane (MJ) McCluskey, York, Pennsylvania: Dear friend, classmate, author of two children's books, and the inspiration that made this book a reality.

Demi Stevens, Year of the Book, Glen Rock, Pennsylvania: This book would not have become all that it is without your belief in me, your consistent nudging along the way, and the countless hours of discussion and editing.

Jean Pierre Michaud, M.D., Caribou, Maine: For teaching me so much about orthopedics in those early years. I'll be forever grateful.

Pat Fallon, M.D., Falmouth, Maine: Your friendship and belief in me gave me the strength to push myself further than I ever thought I could.

Phil Kimball, M.D., Bangor, Maine: For taking me under your wing and helping to navigate the waters as a young salesman.

Steve Rodrigue, M.D., Falmouth, Maine: For putting your trust in me in those first years of your practice when you had so many other choices and for teaching me so much about revision hip surgery.

John West, M.D., Bangor, Maine (Posthumously): For being such a good and loyal customer and friend. I hope you are resting peacefully, my friend.

John Glusic, M.D., Millinocket, Maine: For always being yourself and including me in so many of those special events.

Rejean Label, M.D., Skowhegan, Maine (Posthumously): Our private joke was always that you created a monster. I hope you are resting peacefully, old friend, and smiling down on us.

James Lawsing, M.D.: For putting your trust in me at a time when you had so many other options.

James Curtis, M.D., Bangor, Maine: For your guidance and support. You gave me an opportunity late in your career and it has meant so much to me.

Thanks to Steve deBree, Rick Gerhart, Steve Huff, Andy Kalajian, Bob Leopold, MJ Marasco, Jr., and Bill McCarrick for guidance during the final stages of this publication.

And to the many people too numerous to mention. You put your trust and faith in me along the way and for that I will never forget and will be eternally grateful.

ABOUT THE AUTHOR

GERRY SAVAGE began his sales career over three decades ago in 1985 after serving on active duty in the United States Marines. In 1991 he entered the field of total joint replacement, winning five President Club awards with Zimmer Orthopedics between 1995 and 2003. Gerry went on to become a distributor for Biomet Orthopedics and then eventually served as a Reginal Director for Conformis and Eastern Regional Vice President for MicroPort Orthopedics. Gerry is currently Vice President of Sales for Maxx Orthopedics U.S. He received both his under-graduate and graduate degrees in business administration from Eastern University in St. Davids, Pennsylvania, where he was also an adjunct professor.

When not traveling and pursuing his next opportunity to grow business, Gerry looks forward to spending time in Maine with family and friends, writing with his trusted Cavalier King Charles Spaniel, Brady, by his side, or at the barn riding horses. An avid equestrian, his love for horses was passed down from his grandfather and father. He has competed in the hunter ring over fences as an equestrian throughout central Pennsylvania, where he has lived for the last twelve years with his family.

Made in the USA
Middletown, DE
17 March 2020